BRITISH
MILITARY AIRFIELDS

THEN & NOW

BRITISH
MILITARY AIRFIELDS

THEN & NOW

LEO MARRIOTT

IAN ALLAN Publishing

First published 1997

ISBN 0 7110 2515 0

Published by Ian Allan Publishing

an imprint of Ian Allan Ltd,
Terminal House, Station Approach,
Shepperton, Surrey TW17 8AS.
Printed by Ian Allan Printing Ltd,
at its works at Coombelands in Runnymede, England.

Code 9705/B2

Half title page:
South airfield at the RAF College Cranwell in 1931.
RAF College Cranwell

Title page:
Meteors of Nos 601 and 604 RAuxAF Squadrons at North Weald in 1953. *RAF Museum P100311*

Below:
The Fleet Air Arm Review at Yeovilton in 1964.
QPL F64-29/18

Photographic Notes

The photographs in this book come from a number of sources, the first of which is the Royal Air Force Museum at Hendon. I would like to thank Ray Fennel for his assistance in guiding me through this extensive collection; and Christine Gregory, the photographic manager, for organising the production of the chosen prints. Copies of photographs credited to the museum in this book can be obtained by quoting the reference number given.

A second major source and one which, in my opinion, is sadly under-researched, is the Quadrant Picture Library (credited as QPL) which houses many thousands of photographs taken for *Flight* and *Aeroplane* magazines. I am most grateful to Kathy and Kim for allowing me to spend many interesting hours browsing through piles of fascinating negatives in order to produce a small sample for use in this book. Copies of photos can be obtained by quoting the reference number given to: Quadrant Picture Library, Quadrant House, Sutton, Surrey SM2 5AS.

Photographs from the Fleet Air Arm Museum are credited to FAAM and, again, the negative reference is given in each case.

Many of the photographs of current airfields have come via the Community Relations Officer at the station concerned. Without exception, I have found them to be very courteous and helpful individuals and I thank them heartily for the assistance given and the interest shown. Photographs from these sources are credited to the RAF station concerned.

Photos credited *ASM Photo* are either mine or from my own collection, and others are credited to the individual or organisation named.

CONTENTS

BIBLIOGRAPHY

The Source Book of the RAF, Ken Delve. Airlife, 1994

British Airfield Buildings of the Second World War, Graham Buchan Innes. Midland Publishing Ltd

The Paladins, John James. Macdonald and Co Ltd, 1990

RAF Squadrons, Wg Cdr C. G. Jefford MBE RAF. Airlife, 1988

The Royal Air Force Manual, Tim Laming. Arms & Armour Press, 1994

Squadron Histories. RFC, RNAD & RAF 1912–59, Peter Lewis. Putnam, 1959

British Military Airfields, David J. Smith. Patrick Stephens Ltd, 1989

CFS. Birthplace of Airpower, John W. R. Taylor. Jane's Publishing, 1987

Aircraft of the Royal Air Force Since 1918 (ninth edition), Owen Thetford. Putnam, 1995

British Naval Aircraft Since 1912 (revised edition), Owen Thetford. Putnam, 1978

Military Airfields in the British Isles 1939–1945, S. Willis and B. Holliss. Enthusiast Publications, 1987

In addition to the books mentioned above, a considerable amount of valuable background information was obtained from *Action Stations*, a series in 10 volumes published by Patrick Stephens Ltd and written by several authors including Michael Bowyer, Bruce Barrymore Halpenney, David Smith, Chris Ashworth and Bruce Quarrie.

Other information came from numerous aviation magazines and periodicals of which *Airfield Review*, published quarterly by the Airfield Research Group, was of particular interest.

Left:
The airfield at RAF Shawbury.
Crown Copyright via RAF Shawbury

GLOSSARY

A&AEE	Aircraft and Armament Experimental Establishment		LG	Landing Ground
			MT	Motor Transport
AAC	Army Air Corps		MU	Maintenance Unit
AACU	Anti-Aircraft Co-operation Unit		NAS	Naval Air Squadron
AAP	Aircraft Acceptance Park		NF	Nightfighter
AC	Army Co-operation		OC	Officer Commanding
AEF	Air Experience Flight		OCTU	Officer Cadet Training Unit
AEW	Airborne Early Warning		OCU	Operational Conversion Unit
AFB	Air Force Base (USAF)		OTU	Operational Training Unit
AFDU	Air Fighting Development Unit		PRU	Photographic Reconnaissance Unit
AFS	Advanced Flying School		PSP	Pierced Steel Planking
AMW(C)	Air Mobility Wing (Command)		QRA	Quick Reaction Alert
ANS	Air Navigation School		R	Reserve – when given as a suffix to a squadron number: eg No 20(R)
AOP	Air Observation Post			
ARS	Air Refuelling Squadron (USAF)			
ARW	Air Refuelling Wing (USAF)		RAF	Royal Air Force
ASP	Aircraft Servicing Platform		RAuxAF	Royal Auxiliary Air Force
ASR	Air Sea Rescue		RCAF	Royal Canadian Air Force
ATC	Air Traffic Control		Regt	Regiment
BBMF	Battle of Britain Memorial Flight		REME	Royal Electrical and Mechanical Engineers
C&M	Care and Maintenance: establishments without a role preserved for possible future use			
			RFC	Royal Flying Corps
			RLC	Royal Logistic Corps
CFE	Central Fighter Establishment		RNAS	Royal Naval Air Service
CFS	Central Flying School		RNAY	Royal Naval Aircraft Yard
CN&CS	Central Navigation and Control School		RWR	Radar Warning Receiver
			QRA	Quick Reaction Alert
CO	Commanding Officer		SAC	Strategic Air Command
DERA	Defence Evaluation and Research Agency		SAR	Search and Rescue
			SCR	School of Control and Reporting
EANS	Empire Air Navigation School		SFTS	Service Flying Training School
ECM	Electronic Countermeasures		SHQ	Station Headquarters
EFTS	Elementary Flying Training School		SRW	Strategic Reconnaissance Wing (USAF)
ETPS	Empire Test Pilots' School		STO/VL	Short Take Off/Vertical Landing
ETTF	European Tanker Task Force		TDS	Training Depot Station
EW	Electronic Warfare		TFS	Tactical Fighter Squadron (USAF)
FAA	Fleet Air Arm		TFW	Tactical Fighter Wing (USAF)
FRADU	Fleet Requirements and Aircraft Direction Unit		TOW	Tube-launched Optically-sighted Wire-glided Anti-tank Missile
FTS	Flying Training School		TRW	Tactical Reconnaissance Wing (USAF)
Grp	Group (RAF Formation)			
GRU	General Reconnaissance Unit		TTTE	Tri-National Tornado Training Establishment
GS	General Service (hangar type)			
GSA	Gliding and Soaring Association		TWU	Tactical Weapon Unit
HAS	Hardened Aircraft Shelter		UAS	University Air Squadron
HCU	Heavy Conversion Unit		US	United States
HD	Home Defence		USAAF	United States Army Air Force World War 2 to 1947
HUD	Head Up Display			
IFOR	Implementation Force (NATO Organisation)		USAF	United States Air Force, from 1947
			USAFE	United States Air Forces in Europe
INS	Inertial Navigation System		VGS	Volunteer Gliding School
JATO	Jet-Assisted Take-Off		WAAF	Women's Auxiliary Air Force
JEFTS	Joint Elementary Flying Training School		WRAF	Women's Royal Air Force

INTRODUCTION

In the closing stages of World War 2 there were almost 700 military airfields in the United Kingdom and even in 1918 there were well over 300, although many of the latter were little more than an open field with a few tents and a telephone. Today, by contrast, there are approximately 50 active airfields and less than half of these house major front-line units. It would not be possible in a book of this size to describe and illustrate every airfield which has ever been used for military purposes and, indeed, there are whole series of books which attempt to do this in varying degrees of detail. Instead, this will be a photographic essay on the development of military aviation in this country, seen through the growth and development of its airfields. As far as possible, due prominence will be given to those airfields which continue to play a major role today, but, at the same time, it will not be possible to ignore some famous names from the past which represent airfields now closed or no longer used by the armed forces.

When considering military airfields, thoughts immediately turn to the Royal Air Force which has been the greatest user of airfields since 1918. However, the other services should not be forgotten. The Royal Navy has had its own air arm since 1938 and, before and during World War 1, the Royal Naval Air Service (RNAS) built up a vast organisation of aircraft and airship bases which was absorbed by the fledgling Royal Air Force in 1918. The Army, in the guise of the Royal Flying Corps (RFC), was an equal partner in the formation of the RAF and brought its own infrastructure of airfields to the new service when it was merged with the RNAS. Army flying blossomed again with the formation of an independent Army Air Corps in 1957 and today its units, mostly helicopter-equipped, fly from a number of UK airfields.

It was not only British services which flew from UK airfields. From 1942 the United States Army Air Force (USAAF) quickly built up an enormous presence, mostly at its numerous 8th Air Force bases in East Anglia. Although this quickly reduced at the end of the war, the United States Air Force (as it became in 1947) has continued to. occupy many UK airfields in response to various perceived threats and depending on American policy at the time. Today, following the supposed end of Cold War hostilities with the former Soviet Union, USAF strength is at its lowest and is restricted to only three airfields.

Within the pages of this book will be found examples of all these airfields, together with the men (and women) who worked at and flew from them and, of course, the fascinating and magnificent aircraft which were based thereon. There are many famous airfields, their names known perhaps from the Battle of Britain or the massive and costly bomber campaigns, but there are also many others whose names are not so well known but which performed some function such as training, maintenance or target towing which was vital to the more publicised efforts of the front-line airfields. The reader dipping into these pages will, it is hoped, find examples of all these types of airfields past and present, then and now!

Below:
Leuchars: The coming of jet fighters to Leuchars marked the start of an association which has lasted to the present day. The Meteors of Nos 43 and 222 Squadrons gave way to the graceful swept-wing Hawker Hunter in 1954, while No 151 Squadron, having briefly flown Meteor NF11s, converted to the Venom NF3 also in 1954. Apart from the closure of the airfield for runway lengthening and other improvements, these three squadrons remained together at Leuchars until 1957 when No 222 Squadron disbanded and No 151 re-equipped with Javelins. No 43 Squadron's Hunters left for Cyprus in 1961, but other Javelin squadrons to operate out of Leuchars included Nos 23, 25 and 29.

The Javelin was superseded by the supersonic Lightning in the RAF inventory and it was flown at Leuchars by a number of units including Nos 11, 23, and 74 Squadrons between 1964 and 1975. In the meantime, No 43 Squadron renewed its association with the Scottish airfield when it re-formed here in 1969 with McDonnell Douglas Phantom FG1s, the first RAF Strike Command unit to operate the type as interceptor. When the last of the Lightnings retired in 1975, they were replaced by another Phantom squadron, No 111, and today these two squadrons are still at Leuchars although since 1989 and 1990 respectively they have been flying the Tornado F3.

Shown here is an F3 of No 43 Squadron resplendent in special markings to commemorate the anniversary of the squadron's formation on 15 April 1916; remarkably the squadron has been based at Leuchars for almost half of those 80 years.
Crown Copyright via RAF Leuchars

1 THEN & NOW

The modern military airbase with its acres of concrete, rows of hangars and hardened shelters, a bewildering variety of technical buildings and all the accommodation and facilities of a small town, is a world away from the muddy grass fields with a few wooden sheds and canvas hangars which formed the pioneering airfields before World War 1. In fact, the UK was slow to capitalise on the military value of the Wright Brothers' first manned powered flight in 1903. In Europe the early pacesetters in aviation were the French, while the Germans pioneered the construction of huge and capable rigid airships, the famous Zeppelins, which by 1914 were already capable of carrying up to three tons of bombs and ordnance.

In Britain, the first sustained powered flight by a British-built aircraft was in 1908 when Samuel Cody staggered into the air in a massive kite-like framework nicknamed the 'Cathedral'. Appropriately, the site of this significant event was at Farnborough, Hampshire, which was very much the centre of early pioneering efforts. Originally established in 1905 as a government balloon factory, Farnborough subsequently attracted many private individuals who set up workshops on the edge of Laffans Plain. Later, it became the site of the Government Aircraft Factories which produced such famous aircraft as the BE2C and the SE5 fighter.

The area to the west and south of London was the traditional home of the British Army and the open spaces of Salisbury Plain were extensively used for military training and exercises. Thus when the army became interested in aviation, it was logical that the first sites associated with these activities should be in this area. As early as 1878 the Royal Engineers had experimented with balloons and some had been used in the Boer War. It was the army which had subsidised Cody's efforts to build a successful flying machine, although further allocation of

funds was terminated in 1909. It was not until the following year that all such activity at Farnborough came under the newly designated Army Aircraft Factory, when the Balloon Section at Farnborough was authorised to carry out further investigations into the construction and use of aircraft.

In 1911, military aviation progressed a step further with the formation of the Royal Engineers Air Battalion and, while its newly designated No 1 (Airship) Company remained at Farnborough, a second unit, No 2 (Aeroplane) Company, was set up at Larkhill on Salisbury Plain. Thus Larkhill can be regarded as the very first airfield created for the sole purpose of supporting military fixed-wing flying, although conditions and facilities were extremely primitive. By late summer the Aeroplane Company had eight aircraft on strength as well as a Bleriot XXI owned by one of the pilots. Plans to take part in the army's annual manoeuvres were thwarted when these were cancelled; instead several aircraft were dispatched to temporary landing sites at army training areas at Hardwick, Cambridgeshire, and Thetford, Norfolk. Only two aircraft eventually made the return trip; two others were written off entirely. However, military aviation had at least made a start.

The Royal Navy came into the aviation arena looking for a way to increase the range of its observers and signallers and was kept informed of War Office balloon and airship developments. It became very interested in the possibility of Cody's man-carrying kites as these could be towed behind warships to give the necessary relative wind to sustain them in the air. Trials with modified kites were carried out aboard the cruiser *Hector* and the destroyer *Starfish* as early as 1903 with encouraging results. Cody overplayed his hand by demanding high fees for his continued services and development

temporarily ceased, although four man-carrying kites were purchased. Further kite trials eventually took place in 1908, but by then the Admiralty was convinced of the value of airships for patrol and observation duties and the following year Vickers was awarded a contract to build a rigid airship – the R1. Called *Mayfly*, the R1 was singularly unsuccessful, breaking its back in 1911 while being manoeuvred out of its shed at Vickers' Barrow-in-Furness works. As a result of this disaster, the Naval Airship Section established at Farnborough was closed down the following year.

Fixed-wing naval flying was also slow to start, but in 1911 the Admiralty accepted an offer from a Royal Aero Club member to use his aircraft and the club's facilities at Eastchurch on the Isle of Sheppey for the purpose of teaching naval officers to fly. Subsequently Eastchurch saw more direct military utilisation, but in 1912 the RN established the first of its own airfields on the nearby Isle of Grain although, despite featuring a landing ground, this was mainly intended as a seaplane base. By the following summer, naval coastal seaplane bases had also been established at Calshot, Cromarty, Felixstowe and Great Yarmouth.

In the meantime, military aviation in the United Kingdom was put on a more formalised basis with the establishment of the Royal Flying Corps (RFC) on 13 May 1912. Initially this was organised into separate naval and military wings, an unpopular arrangement which was short-lived, and a fully independent Royal Naval Air Service (RNAS) was eventually formed to take over the duties of the RFC Naval Wing in July 1914. However, one permanent outcome of the formation of the RFC was that the operation of all airships passed to the Naval Wing and subsequently to the RNAS. Another outcome of having a combined RFC was the establishment of the Central Flying School (CFS) at Upavon, Wiltshire, which was intended to train pilots for both parent services. For its time the concept of an inter-service establishment operating a standard training syllabus using the latest contemporary technology was extremely imaginative and innovative – perhaps unconsciously based on the realisation that the aeroplane was going to have a far-reaching impact on the future conduct of war in general and on naval and military operations in particular. Formed at a time when inter-service rivalry was much more common than any form of co-operation, the CFS could well have been a failure. Instead, thanks to the enthusiasm of the early instructors and students from both services, it was extremely successful and eventually became something of an institution in British military flying. Indeed, it is still going strong today, having moved through several other locations since its early days at Upavon.

Thus, by the outbreak of World War 1 in August 1914, the aviation map of Britain was beginning to take shape with RFC bases mainly centred around Salisbury Plain, while the RNAS was flying from coastal bases located mainly in East Anglia, the Medway and on the south coast. However, the next four years would bring about a dramatic and far-reaching expansion of military flying, which would be inevitably accompanied by a staggering increase in the number of UK airfields. Paradoxically, the start of the war was the signal for almost all the RFC's operational strength, some 63 aircraft, to leave for bases in France where they were required to support the British Expeditionary Force then being mobilised and sent across the Channel. All that remained in the UK was the CFS and a few reserve squadrons, and even some of the latter were soon brought up to operational standards and dispatched to France. Losses of pilots, observers and aircraft over the Western Front led almost immediately to an insatiable demand for replacements of both men and aircraft, and this, in turn, set the pattern for the

development of airfields at home. Initially these were mainly training bases, which sprang up all round the country, together with other airfields which acted as aircraft acceptance parks to receive new aircraft from the many manufacturers which came into being, and to prepare these machines for active service. These airfields tended to be near the major industrial cities where aircraft manufacturers had established themselves.

Before the war, little thought had been given to defending Britain against attack from the air, but early Zeppelin raids led to the RNAS initially taking on this role as the RFC was fully committed to the Western Front. It was not until March 1916 that the RFC established permanent Home Defence fighter squadrons. The airfields they used, although rudimentary in the extreme, later expanded and became the sites of many famous Battle of Britain airfields – like Hornchurch and Biggin Hill. However, this was something of a sideshow for the RNAS which concentrated on its primary role of naval co-operation, including the constant patrolling of the sea areas around Great Britain to protect the vital flow of shipping from the ever increasing depredations of the German U-boat fleet. These patrols were flown by a variety of aircraft, but by 1918 the RN had a substantial fleet of multi-engined flying boats such as the Felixstowe F2A, which had an endurance of six hours, carried a crew of four and was armed with several machine guns in addition to carrying a couple of 230lb (104kg) anti-submarine bombs. When comparing this with the flimsy single-engined seaplanes, barely able to lift themselves off the water, with which the RNAS went to war in 1914, the pace of progress was quite staggering. Of course, the increasing sophistication of the aircraft was reflected in the size and complexity of the shore establishments required to support them. Bases such as Felixstowe and Great Yarmouth featured slipways, hardstandings, rows of hangars and specialist workshops, and substantial areas of hutted accommodation for the air and ground crews.

In addition to fixed-wing aircraft, the RN's airships carried a significant proportion of the anti-submarine effort and their bases became major features on the landscape due to the enormous size of the sheds required to house the massive airships. The first naval airship base was at Kingsnorth, Kent, and non-rigids were in action almost immediately in August 1914, helping to escort troop convoys across the channel to France. In 1915 the first purpose-designed Sea Scout (SS) non-rigid airships entered service and were based at Capel (near Folkestone) and Polegate (Eastbourne). Next, in 1916, came the larger Coastal (C) non-rigid airships. New bases to accommodate these and other SS airships were opened in 1916 at Pembroke, Pulham, Howden, Longside, Mullion and East Fortune. The later, and much larger, rigid airships were based mainly at Howden, Pulham and East Fortune. The main advantage of the airship for patrol duties was its exceptional endurance, and the C type regularly completed patrols of 24 hours' duration. After the end of the war, the airship gradually fell out of favour as the performance and versatility of fixed-wing aircraft increased. Although the last naval rigid airship (R34) was not completed until 1919, airship operations were quickly run down after the war and their bases closed or used for other purposes.

From an aviation point of view, the most significant event of 1918 was the amalgamation of the RFC and the RNAS to form the Royal Air Force which, for the next 20 years, became the sole operator of military aircraft for the British armed forces. The setting up of an independent air force was a far-reaching step which had been precipitated mainly by the problems encountered in trying to organise an effective defence of Britain against attack by both Zeppelins and fixed-wing aircraft, notably the efficient Gotha twin-engined bombers which enjoyed some spectacular successes including the daylight bombing of London in 1917. However, with the end of hostilities in November 1918, there was an immediate move to slash the size (and expense) of Britain's armed forces and the RAF was lucky to survive, particularly as the RN began to realise the implications of allowing its air power to be run by another service and began a relentless campaign to disband the RAF and regain its own air service. Although it eventually achieved the latter aim in 1938, the RAF managed to survive as a separate entity almost entirely due to the efforts of one man – Air Marshal Sir Hugh Trenchard, known for good reason as the 'father' of the Royal Air Force.

Nevertheless there were extensive cuts. The number of airfields used by the RAF dwindled to a mere handful and by 1921 the total front-line strength consisted of less than 30 squadrons, compared to over 200 at the end of the war. Over half of these were based overseas, mostly in the Middle East or India where the fledgling service was carving a role for itself attempting to keep the peace amongst the warring factions within the many countries and territories which comprised the British Empire. At home there were only two fighter and two bomber squadrons, another two squadrons tasked with army co-operation, and a total of five squadrons employed on naval-related duties. Even including training, experimental and flying boat bases, there were only 22 fully operational airfields in use. At the same time there

was some rationalisation of the RAF command structure which would in turn affect the use and development of airfields within the UK. Initially the country had been divided up into several operational areas, but, with the rapid contraction of the air force, in 1919 these were rationalised into two – Northern and Southern. At the same time, the Coastal Area was formed with responsibility for all air units operating with the RN in home waters (eventually this would include aircraft embarked aboard ships). The Northern and Southern areas were amalgamated in 1920 to become the Inland Area so that all operational RAF aircraft in the UK came under one of two commands: Inland or Coastal. During the late 1920s and early 1930s, the Inland Area underwent a series of reorganisations and its subdivisions included the Fighting Area and Wessex Bombing Area as well as an Air Defence Group responsible for the various Auxiliary and Reserve squadrons. In 1936 a more fundamental reorganisation took place when the well-known Command system came into being with Fighter, Bomber and Training Commands being created from various functions of the Inland Area while the Coastal Area became Coastal Command.

A look at the dispositions of the few operational squadrons during this period will give some idea of the airfields in use at the time. In 1922 there were bombers squadrons based at Spittlegate, Bircham Newton and Kenley; a single fighter squadron at Hawkinge; army co-operation squadrons at Farnborough and Digby; Coastal Area land-based aircraft at Gosport and Leuchars. In addition, there were flying boat units at Felixstowe, Calshot and Plymouth. Ten years later, following a modest increase in strength but before the major expansion programmes of the mid and late 1930s, the number of active airfields had increased to around 57. Of these there were seven operational stations in the Wessex Bombing Area (Andover, Bicester, Bircham Newton, Boscombe Down, Netheravon, Upper Heyford and

Worthy Down), and another seven in the Fighting Area (Biggin Hill, Duxford, Hawkinge, Hornchurch, Northolt, Tangmere and Upavon). RAuxAF squadrons were at Manston, Filton, Aldergrove, Waddington, Hucknall, Hendon, Renfrew, Turnhouse, Castle Bromwich, Usworth and Thornaby, while training establishments under the Inland Area accounted for another 12 airfields. Coastal Area aircraft operated from four airfields (Donibristle, Leuchars, Gosport and Lee-on-Solent) and four flying boat bases.

One of Trenchard's major and lasting achievements was the early foundation of training establishments where the highest standards were expected and obtained. The RAF College opened at Cranwell in 1920 (together with the School of Technical Training for boy mechanics), while No 1 School of Technical Training opened at Halton in the same year. In 1924 the School of Aeronautical Engineering opened at Henlow for the purpose of providing technical and engineering courses for officers – one famous graduate was a Flg Off Whittle who would make his name as the inventor of the jet engine. In 1947 Henlow was renamed the RAF Technical College; it continued at the same site until amalgamated with the RAF College at Cranwell in 1965.

The lead up to World War 2 was perhaps the most important part of the story of Britain's airfields as the ever accelerating expansion programmes from 1934 led to a major increase in buildings and facilities at existing airfields and the opening and construction of many more. As a new service, the RAF sought to build up its corporate identity by employing the major architects and planners of the times, such as Lutyens and Archibald, to design and plan the buildings and layout of its permanent establishments. A typical example was the RAF College at Cranwell, built in the early 1930s and which, capped with its impressive dome visible for miles around, sought to emulate the older, rival establishments at Sandhurst and Dartmouth. The 1930s' expansion programme laid great emphasis on the provision of permanent airfields – which could take up to four years to build – because aircraft to fly from them could be assembled relatively quickly. Initially all these bases were built around grass aerodromes, but usually with a paved perimeter track. Centrepiece of the whole layout was a number of imposing hangars (usually the well known C type) in which the squadrons' aircraft could be housed, maintained and repaired. However, a major airfield could be manned by hundreds, even thousands of airmen and women, all of whom had to be accommodated and fed. Lutyens went into great detail in designing everything including the officers' mess, married quarters, guardhouses, airmen's accommodation blocks, canteens, NAAFI buildings, stores, repair shops and a whole range

Opposite:
The first significant expansion of British airfields after World War 1 occurred in the early 1920s when it was realised that the RAF was totally outnumbered by the French Air Force. Many airfields were upgraded and this Type A hangar at Netheravon is a typical structure of the period. *ASM Photo*

Below:
The most significant event in the history of British military airfields was the expansion programme of the 1930s. This view of RAF Leeming nearing completion in 1939 illustrates the effect achieved by designing new airfields from scratch so that they could be built to an overall plan and standardised layout.
RAF Leeming Photographic Section

of minor buildings. Amazingly, virtually all of these are still standing today, still used for the purpose for which they were designed and built over 60 years ago. In terms of practicality and durability, considering the rate of technological change, they must represent some of the best architectural investment ever made.

Work on the first new expansion programme airfields began in 1935 and among these were Thorney Island, Odiham, Harwell, Marham, Stradishall, Waddington, Feltwell, Cranfield, Manby, Church Fenton and Ternhill. Existing stations, including Catterick, Cranwell, Halton, Hornchurch, Tangmere and Wittering, also began a full scale modernisation at the same time. In the following year work began on several new airfields which were to become well known, including Dishforth, Driffield, Finningley, Leconfield, Scampton and Wyton. The disposition of these and subsequent airfields recognised that the threat came from Germany, so they were sited to defend London and the Midlands from attacks across the North Sea, and to provide bases in East Anglia, Lincolnshire and Yorkshire for bombers to reach out in the reverse direction. In the late 1930s there were no less than eight separate expansion programmes proposed, including three in 1938 alone, but when war broke out in 1939 most of these were a long way from completion. The original Scheme A, put forward in 1934, provided for a front-line strength of 960 aircraft organised into 76 squadrons by early 1939, while the last, Scheme M dating from 1938, increased this to 1,360 aircraft in 145 squadrons, to be implemented by 1942. A total of 46 airfields were approved for construction or modernisation to house this force.

In 1937, just before World War 2 started, the Admiralty had at last achieved its ambition to have control of its own air arm and it immediately inherited four airfields from the RAF, these being Donibristle near the naval base at Rosyth on the Firth of Forth, Lee-on-Solent, Gosport and Worthy Down, all adjacent to the Portsmouth naval base. Early in 1939 it also took over the civil airfield at Eastleigh and the former Coastal Area airfield at Ford in Sussex. The first purpose-built Naval Air Station (NAS) was at Hatson in the Orkneys; officially opened in October 1939, its task was to provide a base for the air defence of the important fleet anchorage at Scapa Flow. Other naval airfields were built at Yeovilton, Crail, Arbroath and St Merryn, all being operational by the end of 1940. During the war, the Fleet Air Arm expanded out of all recognition and was still expanding in 1945 in anticipation of being involved in a protracted Pacific war. At one stage the RN operated from almost 50 airfields in the UK, and its operational and training units also flew from many RAF bases at various times.

The predictable increase in the number of airfields was given a dramatic boost in 1942 following the entry of the United States into the fray against Germany. Eager to join the fray against Germany, the first USAAF units arrived in June 1942 and by the end of the year there were four B-17 Flying Fortress and two B-24 Liberator groups, together with a few fighter groups flying the P-38 Lightning. These aircraft, and their successors, were almost all based at airfields in East Anglia, in a few cases taking over airfields such as Bassingbourn and Lakenheath which the RAF had already built and developed under the prewar expansion plans. However, with typical American zeal and drive, the USAAF quickly embarked on an airfield construction programme of its own which rapidly eclipsed anything which had gone before. The displaced

RAF squadrons were redeployed and the whole of the east coast from Teesside to the Thames became the springboard for the ever growing bomber offensive against Germany. By 1944, Bomber Command was organised into six groups of which two were in East Anglia, including Cambridgeshire, two in Lincolnshire and two in Yorkshire.

Earlier in the war, attention had concentrated more on fighter dispositions as Britain fought for its very existence in the Battle of Britain and then attempted to counter the menace of the night bomber during the Blitz raids of 1941. As much of the German effort was directed against south-east England and London, the disposition of the defences naturally reflected this. Airfields in Essex, Kent and Surrey bore the brunt of the fighting at this stage of the war, but other parts of the United Kingdom were not neglected and adequate fighter defences were stationed to cover major industrial cities and important military concentrations. In general, training units were based on the west side of the country, so as to be less

liable to attack and also to avoid conflicting with operational units. However, there were operational bases on the west coast – the many Coastal Command bases in Cornwall, Northern Ireland and Scotland where aircraft were needed to operate over the vast expanses of the Atlantic Ocean, protecting the convoys which were vital to Britain's continuation of the war.

At the peak of the air effort, in late 1944, there were almost 700 airfields in use within the UK, but, as the tide of war swept on to continental Europe and the end of the fighting became a predictable event, some airfields then fell into disuse. With the end of hostilities in 1945, the closure of airfields accelerated and many were quickly released for other uses, their temporary buildings being dismantled, left to decay, or sometimes being put to a variety of peaceful uses. However, the permanent stations which had been solidly constructed before the war generally remained as active RAF stations and the peacetime RN still had use for a significant number of airfields. The rapid decline in the strength of the armed forces was halted with the onset of the Cold War and the crisis of the Berlin Airlift in 1948. The Korean War started in 1950 and throughout the following decade there was a very real fear that a war with the Soviet Union could break out at any time.

Opposite:
Then – the Operations Room at RAF Leeming in 1941.
RAF Leeming Photographic Section

Above:
Now – Approach Control Room at RNAS Culdrose.
Crown Copyright via RNAS Culdrose

As the RAF and RN assessed their requirements for the new threat, there were many new factors to take into account when planning the disposition and equipping of airfields. Thanks to the legacy of World War 2, there were plenty of airfields available and no new ones were built. However, these airfields had not been designed to cope with the requirements of jet aircraft which, having first entered operational service in 1944, had virtually replaced piston-engined aircraft in front-line service by 1950. On top of this, in the decade which followed, guided missiles began to emerge as a possible substitute for the manned aircraft. Above all, of course, hung the threat of the atomic bomb and the horrors of nuclear warfare. The new face of air warfare was reflected in the number and types of airfields used by the RAF. A policy of nuclear deterrence based on the new V-Force (Valiant, Vulcan and Victor) entailed an expensive refurbishment of many airfields so that they could operate the new four-engined jet bombers. Apart from obvious work, like extending and strengthening runways, other requirements included new workshop and maintenance facilities, dispersed parking bays and Quick Reaction Alert (QRA) pads, new ATC and communications facilities and, last but not least, facilities for storing and handling the nuclear weapons which the bombers would carry. V-bomber bases included Finningley, Scampton, Waddington, Cottesmore, Gaydon, Honington, Wittering and Wyton. By the early 1960s the RAF also deployed several squadrons of American-built Thor ICBMs, sited on old World War 2 airfields such as Carnaby, Hemswell, Ludford Magna, Feltwell, Mepal and Folkingham. In addition, the defence of the Thor and V-bomber bases relied in part on batteries of Bloodhound surface-to-air missiles. Some of these were sited at separate locations such as North Coates, Dunholme Lodge and Rattlesden, but others were alongside operational airfields such as

Marham and Watton. Fighter defences relied increasingly on two-seat all-weather aircraft, initially the Meteor NF variants and then the delta-winged Javelin, and these were deployed along a string of east coast airfields including Leuchars, Middleton St George, Leconfield, Coltishall and Wattisham.

In the 1960s the RN still had a powerful FAA operating from eight carriers. To support this activity it maintained air bases at Lossiemouth, Culdrose, Brawdy, Yeovilton, Lee-on-Solent and Portland. However, the demise of the conventional fixed-wing carriers in the early 1970s led to the RAF taking over Brawdy and Lossiemouth and today naval aviation is concentrated at Yeovilton and Culdrose. Lee-on-Solent has closed and Portland is due to close by 1999.

The Cold War era also produced another change in British military aviation when the Army Air Corps (AAC) was formally constituted in 1957 and became responsible for operating helicopters and light aircraft in direct support of the army – this had been a function of the RAF's AOP squadrons. The new corps set up its headquarters at Middle Wallop, which continues today as the centre of army aviation. Initially the army operated few airfields of its own but in recent years the increasing importance of the helicopter on the battlefield has led to concepts such as the Airmobile Brigade and the sophisticated Apache dedicated anti-tank helicopter. To support these changes the AAC now runs a number of airfields including Dishforth and Wattisham.

Changing priorities and a gradual withdrawal of

Above:
This airmen's accommodation block at Wittering was built in the 1920s but survives in good condition today, still used for its original purpose. *ASM Photo*

Right:
Expansion programme architecture – 1. A group commander's house, RAF Leeming. *ASM Photo*

Top:
Expansion programme architecture – 2. Officer's married quarters house, RAF Leeming. *ASM Photo*

Above:
Expansion programme architecture – 3. A fine example of an officers' mess, RAF Benson. *ASM Photo*

Top:
Today's architecture – airmen's married quarters, RAF Leeming. *ASM Photo*

Above:
Old and New. A brand-new hangar built to accommodate AAC helicopters stands alongside the 1930s C type hangar, still in use, at Wattisham.
ASM Photo

16

British forces from overseas bases led inevitably to a contraction of the RAF during the 1970s and 1980s, and the closure and disposal of many airfields and other establishments. Some long-serving and famous airfields fell victim to successive defence reviews, including Biggin Hill, Bassingbourn, Little Rissington, Hullavington and Upwood. Today the operational front line strength of the RAF is housed in only a dozen or so airfields, but each of these is home to several squadrons and boasts the sophisticated facilities required to service and fly complex modern combat aircraft. It is, however, sobering to think that the fighter defence of the UK now depends on only three airfields (Leuchars, Leeming and Coningsby) which between them operate the six squadrons of Tornado F3s responsible for the protection of British airspace. Strike squadrons are based at Coltishall (Jaguars), Marham and Lossiemouth (Tornados) and Wittering (Harriers) while maritime patrol Nimrods fly from Kinloss. Helicopters and transport squadrons are based at Odiham, Benson, Brize Norton and Lyneham. There are, of course, other airfields – mainly concerned with training and second-line duties – but the grand total of active military airfields in the UK is now about only 50. It remains to be seen whether the minimum has been reached or if there are further cuts and reductions to come. At the time of writing there are signs that a period of relative stability has been reached and once the provisions of the recent 'Options for Defence' review have been fully implemented it is possible that the number of active airfields will remain constant for some time to come. Time alone will tell!

Below:
A memorial park at RAF Lakenheath serves as a reminder of the USAF forces based here and the lives lost in the cause of peace. *ASM Photo*

Above:
Then – a Handley Page Victor of No 10 Squadron undergoes a major check in one of Cottesmore's C type hangars in 1958. *QPL 37917S*

Below:
Now – Tornados of the TTTE are serviced in the same hangar today. *ASM Photo*

Above right:
E-3D Sentries lined up in front of their purpose-built hangar at Waddington. *RAF Waddington*

Below right:
A view over the airfield from the Visual Control Room at RNAS Culdrose.
Crown Copyright via RNAS Culdrose

2 THE CRADLE

Left:

Leysdown: The flat marshy landscape on the eastern side of the Isle of Sheppey was a natural site for the endeavours of the early British aviators as it was free of obstructions which might endanger aircraft in flight, offered flat fields for take-off and landing, and was sparsely inhabited so that the many crashes and unscheduled landings were unlikely to cause damage to other persons or property. It was also relatively near London and so it was to Leysdown that members of the Aero Club (later to become the Royal Aero Club) came in 1909 and bought 400 acres (162ha) of land to create Britain's first genuine airfield. In association with the Aero Club, the Short brothers – Oswald, Eustace and Horace – also purchased some land and quickly erected sheds and workshops where they started to build under licence an initial batch of six Wright Flyer biplanes. This was the world's first ever aeroplane production contract and the site at Leysdown was visited by the Wright brothers in May 1909.

However, such was the pace of progress that the Leysdown airfield, with its numerous dykes and ditches presenting dangerous hazards, was quickly seen to be unsuitable for further development and the Aero Club moved to a new site at nearby Eastchurch early in 1910. It was followed by the Short brothers and their factory by April of the same year. This was not quite the end of Leysdown which, during World War 1, was used as a satellite to Eastchurch and by 1918 was home to the Pilots' and Observers' Aerial Gunnery and Aerial Fighting School. Students carried out classroom training at Eastchurch and moved to Leysdown for practical exercises in firing and bomb dropping, the open tidal reaches of the Thames estuary being an ideal area for such activities. An official report at that time stated that the airfield occupied 115 acres (47ha) with maximum dimensions of 1,100yd by 700yd (1,000m by 640m). Buildings included three large aeroplane sheds (probably the old Shorts factory buildings) and three Bessonneaux canvas hangars. When the war ended, all facilities at Leysdown were withdrawn and although used occasionally as a practice landing ground in the interwar years, it saw no further use after the outbreak of World War 2 in 1939.

This aerial view shows the site of the airfield as it is today. In the foreground is the beach and shoreline, while the house in the left background is Muswell ('Mussel' in contemporary documents) Manor, which was purchased by the Aero Club for use by its members; both the Short and Wright brothers stayed there in 1909 along with other notable names from British aviation history including Moore Brabazon and Charles Rolls. *ASM Photo*

Right:

Eastchurch: Located only a few miles to the west of Leysdown, but, being slightly higher above sea level, the land was better drained and provided a better surface for flying operations. Hangars, stores and workshops quickly sprang up on rising ground bordering the north side of the airfield following the first aircraft landing at Eastchurch in November 1909. The next year saw great progress with several pioneering milestones being passed, including a long-distance flight by Tommy Sopwith (another legendary name) to Thirlemont in Belgium. During this time the RN had kept a watching brief on activity at Eastchurch as it was only a few miles from the then important bases at Sheerness and Chatham and in February 1911 the Admiralty accepted an offer by Frank McClean of the Royal Aero Club to provide facilities for four naval officers to be taught to fly, the course beginning on 2 March. One of the officers to graduate was Lt Samson who subsequently persuaded the Admiralty to purchase its own aeroplanes and set up an official naval flying school at Eastchurch. This was duly done and the airfield was rented to the RN who subsequently requisitioned it shortly after the outbreak of war in 1914. By that time Shorts had

established an excellent relationship with the navy and went on to supply it with hundreds of aircraft including the first successful torpedo bomber – the Type 184 floatplane which was credited with the first sinking of a ship by aerial torpedo attack, during the Dardanelles campaign of 1915. Eastchurch was also a centre for trials and development including experiments with rocket projectiles and the fitting of wireless sets to naval aircraft.

This photo, taken at Eastchurch in 1917, shows a selection of naval training aircraft standing in front of one of the hangars. In the foreground is a Fowzey Farman, a development of the primitive Maurice Farman Shorthorn with an enclosed nacelle to accommodate the pilots, while on the right is one of 85 American-built Curtiss R-2s. The latter would also have been used to train American pilots as their forces began to enter the European conflict in 1917. By 1918 Eastchurch was home to an Observers' School, a Ground Armament School and a Boy Mechanics' School as well as its original Flying School, but, despite being mainly concerned with training, Eastchurch saw action on several occasions, being involved in attempts (unsuccessful) to intercept airship and aircraft raids. *RAF Museum P016198*

Right:

Eastchurch: This aerial view, probably taken in 1918, is oriented with north at the top of the picture and shows the layout of the airfield with the main camp in the centre, six large hangars to the east, and numerous small aeroplane sheds to south. Most of the latter were the original buildings erected by the Aero Club and the Short brothers, while the larger hangars were built by the RN during the war. The actual aerodrome stretches away to the east and south of the hangar lines. *FAAM A/STN 301*

Left:

Eastchurch: After the Armistice in 1918, Eastchurch was reduced to C&M status, but in 1922 it formally reopened as an Armament and Gunnery School and continued in this role until well into World War 2. At the same time various operational squadrons, including Nos 33 and 207, were based here and in 1940 the airfield became part of No 16 Group, Coastal Command. During the Battle of Britain it was attacked several times and sustained significant damage. By August 1941 the airfield had reverted to the training role although it was still used occasionally for operational tasks, notably by the Spitfires of Nos 65 and 165 Squadrons in support of the costly Dieppe operation in August 1942. In the latter part of the war Eastchurch housed the centralised Personnel Reselection Centre, the last service unit to occupy the airfield which was reduced to C&M in 1946 when the centre closed. RAF occupation ended in 1948 and in 1950 the airfield became the site for a prison, a role it fulfils today. Two large purpose-built modern complexes cover much of the land that was previously part of the airfield, but among the prison amenities is an extensive farm which is worked by the inmates.

As this photo shows, some of the farm sheds in use today date from the aviation activities of World War 1. The one in the centre is almost certainly the same one that features in the 1917 photo, while the row of black-roofed sheds behind it can be identified among the southern line of sheds in the 1918 aerial photo! *ASM Photo*

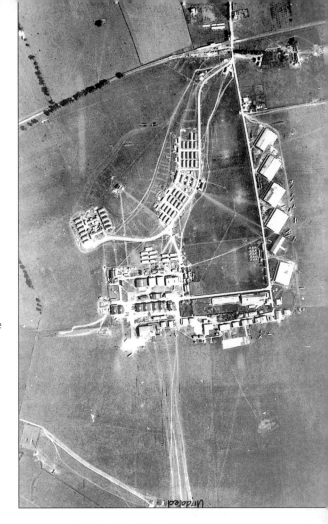

Below:
Larkhill: While the RN developed its interest in aviation on the Isle of Sheppey, it was natural that the army should concentrate its activities within its traditional training area, the rolling downs of Salisbury Plain. The first powered aeroplane to fly in Britain was actually financed by the War Office and was designated British Army Aeroplane No 1. Built at Farnborough, then the base of the Royal Engineers Balloon Company, by the famous Samuel Cody, it took to the air in September 1908. However, it did not lead directly to operational military aircraft and, as in the RN, it was left to individual officers to pursue their interest in flying and demonstrate the practicality of the new invention. As a result, it was not until February 1911 that the Air Battalion, Royal Engineers, was set up with No 1 (Balloon) Company remaining at Farnborough and provision for the establishment of No 2 (Aeroplane) Company to be based at Larkhill on Salisbury Plain where the Bristol and Colonial Aeroplane Co had already established an airfield on 2,284 acres (914ha) of land leased from the War Office in 1910. The enterprising Bristol Co had already erected several sheds to be used for the building of aircraft, including the famous Bristol Boxkite copied from the French Henri Farman design; in addition, the company had established a flying school where several army officers learnt to fly.

This photograph shows a Bristol-built Prier Dickson monoplane originally delivered to the Aeroplane Company at Larkhill in 1912 and later used by No 3 Squadron.
Museum of Army Flying

Right:
Larkhill: This otherwise unremarkable field, just off the A360 Salisbury-Devizes road near Stonehenge, is part of the site of the first official British military airfield. A nearby monument records the death of an officer in a 1913 air crash and the road junction is still known as Airmen's Corner. As the Aeroplane Company was billeted in tents and the aircraft housed in canvas hangars, there are no permanent remains visible today. Despite its significance, the airfield had a

relatively short history, its highlight being the first military aircraft trials held here in August 1912, but with the development of nearby Upavon and Netheravon, army activity tailed off and the Bristol Co closed down its school in June 1914. Since that time army co-operation aircraft have flown from various temporary strips in the Larkhill area, and an RAF Larkhill existed at nearby Knighton Down between 1936 and the middle of World War 2 when it became War Office property again. *ASM Photo*

Left:
Larkhill: Early aviation was a dangerous activity and this stone cross near the original Larkhill airfield stands today as a memorial to Maj Alexander William Hewetson of the Royal Field Artillery, who was killed when his aircraft crashed here in July 1913. *ASM Photo*

Below:
Larkhill: The most tangible remaining association with the original airfield is the Bustard Inn, a mile or so from the site of the airfield and the place where the officers of No 2 Company were billeted due to the lack of any other suitable accommodation. One can only assume that the early aviators found some consolation in being forced to live in a pub! On the top of the hill in the background can be seen the balloon sheds of Rollestone Camp, which was established in 1916 to house No 1 Balloon School, although these present sheds were not actually built until 1932 when they replaced the fragile Bessonneaux canvas hangars previously in use. *ASM Photo*

Netheravon: Activity began to decline at Larkhill as the neighbouring airfield at Netheravon was developed. This was based on a camp previously occupied by a cavalry school and the airfield consisted of open stretches of rolling grassland, ideal for riding but an unlikely spot for flying activities. Nevertheless, Netheravon can today claim to be the oldest operational military airfield in the country, having been in almost continuous use since 1913 when No 3 Squadron RFC moved here from Larkhill. In the summer of 1914 the army held a concentration camp at which the whole of the military wing of the RFC was assembled to exercise the fledgling organisation as it prepared for the impending war. When this broke out in August 1914, virtually every serviceable aeroplane set off for France, leaving only a few training aircraft and a couple of partially formed squadrons. Netheravon was used by No 1 Squadron in a training role

until 1915, after which the airfield became a centre for the preparation and dispatch of aircraft to France. Later in the war it reverted to the training role as the need for replacement pilots rapidly outstripped supply. By 1918 the airfield housed Nos 8 and 12 Training Depot Stations, which were responsible for both basic and advanced training and flew a wide variety of aircraft types including the massive Handley Page O/400. After the Armistice, the various training units briefly disbanded, but in December 1919 No 1 FTS was established and subsequently became responsible for training FAA pilots, a task which continued, on and off, until March 1942.

Shown here is an Avro 504K of 1 FTS coming into land on the hilltop airfield at Netheravon at some time in the early 1920s, while the camp buildings can be seen sloping away in the background. *RAF Museum P11705*

Netheravon: An aerial view taken in 1928 showing the main camp and one of the Type A hangars at the western end of the airfield. The main section of the landing area was to the east of this site and included another two Type A hangars as well as a 'Cathedral' type. During World War 2 the airfield became a training centre for airborne forces and from late 1941 it was used for glider pilot training by No 296 Squadron using Hectors and Harts to tow Hotspur gliders and by No 297 Squadron to carry out parachute training with converted Whitley bombers. Subsequently the larger Horsa and Hamilcar gliders made their appearance as the training tempo increased in preparation for D-Day in June 1944, but thereafter the workload ran down, being mainly concerned with glider repair, maintenance and various trials and tests. Despite its undulating grass surface, the airfield had been used at various times by many types of heavy aircraft including Whitleys, Halifaxes and Stirlings. *RAF Museum P1017409*

Above:
Netheravon: Towards the end of World War 2 Netheravon was transferred to Transport Command and until 1948 some glider and parachute training continued. Thereafter operational flying more or less ceased and the camp was used by the RAF Police as their headquarters and training depot until they left in 1960. The airfield was then officially closed and although army-related recreational flying started up in 1963, it was not until 1966 that Netheravon became an operational airfield again when the expanding AAC took it over, making it an HQ for all operational AAC aircraft while Middle Wallop concentrated on training activities. Today major units have relocated to other AAC airfields but it is still used by 7 Regiment, AAC, with two TA squadrons flying Gazelles as tasked by GOC UK Land Forces. One of these is shown parked in front of one of the A type hangars, all of which still survive, although this example has had modern offices and workshops grafted on to the side. *ASM Photo*

Right:
Netheravon: The whole camp and airfield is in something of a time warp. Although facilities have been modernised at Netheravon and there has been some new construction, most of the original buildings dating from around 1913 are intact and in daily use. Perhaps the most striking of these is the officers' mess which still proudly displays the Royal Flying Corps wings above its front entrance. *ASM Photo.*

29

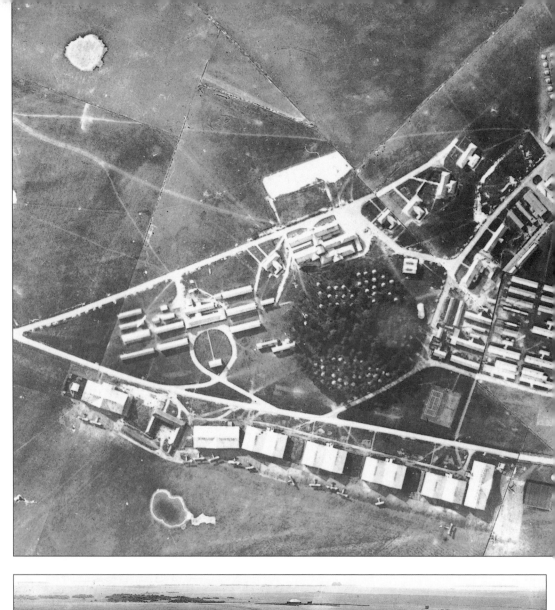

international centre of excellence in the years to come. The outbreak of World War 1 in 1914 led to the departure of almost all the aircraft and pilots, and the CFS at Upavon subsequently became merely one of many centres for advanced training, although in 1915 the Experimental Flight was formed to test prototypes of new aircraft. This important work grew to such an extent that in 1917 the flight was transferred to Martlesham Heath where it became the Aircraft and Armament Experimental Establishment (A&AEE).

This view of Upavon was taken in 1918 when the airfield was at its wartime peak, having grown from its original 2,400 acres (972ha) to cover a total area of 3,324 acres (1,305ha), and shows the airfield divided by the main Andover-Devizes road (now the A342) which runs from right to left through the lower half of the picture. The main camp is in the centre, while lines of hangars and numerous aircraft can be seen on the south (lower) and east (right) sides.
RAF Museum P004738

Far left:
Upavon: After World War 1, the CFS was run down until it was reopened in 1920 as a centre for training flying instructors using the methods pioneered by Smith-Barry at Gosport and was equipped with Avro 504s and Sopwith Snipes. In 1924 it moved to Wittering and Upavon became a No 3 Group station, housing Nos 3 and 17 Fighter Squadrons. These subsequently moved to Kenley in 1934 and, after a short period as an FAA base, the airfield saw the return of the CFS at the end of 1935. By now the school was flying Tutors, Harts and Furies, and later operated twin-engined Ansons and Oxfords as well. Improvements to the station buildings were undertaken in 1938 as part of the expansion scheme, including the erection of one of the ubiquitous C type hangars.

This photo was taken in 1938 and shows several of the CFS Avro Tutors with a Hawker Hart taxying out in the left background. Pressures of war led to a mushrooming of the RAF's flying training programme and the CFS gradually lost its unique status until it was formally disbanded in 1942 and its staff absorbed into No 7 Flying Instructors School which remained at Upavon until April 1946. *QPL 16027S*

Above:
Upavon: At the end of 1911 a sub-committee of the Committee of Imperial Defence investigated the progress of military aviation to date and attempted to establish a framework for the future development and application of air power to naval and military operations. Out of their deliberations came recommendations which resulted in the establishment of the Royal Flying Corps with naval and military wings and the setting up of the Central Flying School to ensure a supply of properly trained pilots to the new formations.

The chosen site for the CFS was Upavon in Wiltshire, only a few miles north of Netheravon. Like its neighbour, it was on undulating, hilly land which had previously been used as training gallops and was totally unsuitable for the frail aircraft of the time. CFS opened in June 1912, at which time it had only seven aircraft – two Farmans, two Shorts, two Avros and a Bristol biplane. Under its first commandant, Capt Godfrey Paine RN, the school began to build up a reputation for thoroughness and efficiency which was to make it an

Top:
Upavon: With the cessation of flying training, activity at the airfield was largely limited to communications duties by aircraft attached to the various group and command headquarters which moved into Upavon. Initially there was No 38 Group, Transport Command, which specialised in tactical co-operation with the army, and in 1950 Transport Command headquarters moved here, remaining in residence throughout its transmutations into Air Support Command in 1967 and later as No 46 Group which took over the ASC function when the latter was absorbed into Strike Command in 1972. Upavon continued as an RAF headquarters until the early 1990s when control of all groups reverted to Strike Command headquarters at High Wycombe. The airfield and camp were transferred in 1993 to the army which has now located several administrative headquarters in the former RAF facilities including HQ Provost Marshal's Department,

HQ Adjutant General's Department, and various training functions.

A visible reminder of the past is this hut, known as the Trenchard building, which was the original CFS headquarters in 1912 and now houses a small museum illustrating the history of RAF Upavon and its association with the CFS. On the left can be seen a small section of the large administration complex built in the 1950s to accommodate RAF Transport Command HQ. *ASM Photo*

Above:
Upavon: The airfield at Upavon is virtually unused today, the only movements being the occasional training flight by Hercules based at Lyneham, but everything is kept neat and tidy. This current view shows the small control tower which stands in front of one of two A type hangars erected in the 1920s, and a single C type hangar is on the right. *ASM Photo*

Below:

Gosport: The traditional high standards of British military pilots are firmly based on the foundations of the work carried out by the CFS in its early days, and on the work of one of its earliest students, Col Robert Smith-Barry RFC. After passing out from the first CFS course in 1912 he subsequently fought with the RFC in France and was appalled at the lack of skill and enthusiasm shown by newly trained replacement pilots sent out to the squadrons during 1916. When he returned to England at the end of that year he was given command of No 1 Reserve Squadron at Gosport and proceeded to introduce a then revolutionary system of flying training involving the use of proper dual control aircraft and a series of set exercises and lessons intended to give students a proper understanding of the nature of each manoeuvre and the correct method of carrying it out. The properly structured course consisted of periods of dual instruction followed by confidence-building sessions of solo practice and consolidation before moving on to the next stage. Although this might seem obvious today, it was startlingly new for its time and the 'Smith-Barry' method was adopted as standard by the CFS which then ensured that all instructors were taught its proper application.

The airfield at Gosport was first established by the RFC in 1914 and was situated on flat ground just outside the defensive perimeter constituted in Victorian times to defend the land approaches to the Portsmouth dockyard and naval base. It was overlooked by two solid forts (Fort Rowner and Fort Grange) whose dank and musty depths provided some accommodation for the early aviators. Canvas hangars were erected for the aircraft but these were gradually replaced by more substantial sheds during World War 1. At first the airfield acted as a base for the formation of squadrons prior to their dispatch to France and an excellent account of the airfield at that time, including a poignant description of a squadron departing for France, is given in the opening chapters of Cecil Lewis's famous book *Sagittarius Rising*. However, by the time Smith-Barry arrived in 1916 the airfield was almost totally given over to flying training and the following year his School of Special Flying was set up by the amalgamation of Nos 1, 25 and 55 Training Squadrons, a line-up of the school's Avro 504s being shown here. Other training units also used the airfield and it remained responsible for the aerial defence of the Portsmouth area until the end of the war in 1918.
RAF Museum P019812

Above:
Gosport: In 1919 the airfield was allocated to the RAF's Coastal Area and became the base for a number of units and flights employed on naval duties. In particular, Gosport became home to the Development Flight which was responsible for testing aircraft and equipment for the torpedo-dropping role, and training crews in the relevant tactics and techniques. During the interwar years a succession of torpedo bombers could be seen at Gosport, including the Blackburn Dart, Baffin and Shark, and the famous Fairey Swordfish. During this period four A type hangars were constructed, followed by a single C type, and two short paved runways were laid down to provide a facility for practising carrier landings.

Two of the hangars can be seen in this 1935 photo which shows over 90 aircraft lined up in preparation for the Silver Jubilee Review of the Fleet in 1935. From right to left the rows of aircraft include: Blackburn Sharks, Blackburn Baffins, three rows of Hawker Nimrods and Ospreys, three rows of Fairey Seals and IIIFs and another row of unidentified torpedo bombers. However, despite the airfield's naval connections, it was not handed over to the Admiralty in 1937 following the establishment of an independent Fleet Air Arm but remained an RAF station (in name at least) until after the end of World War 2. *FAAM A/STN 30*

Left:
Gosport: Plan of the aerodrome showing its layout prior to the extension of the landing runs in 1940. The original runways shown here were laid down in the 1930s to allow carrier deck landings to be practised. *FAAM*

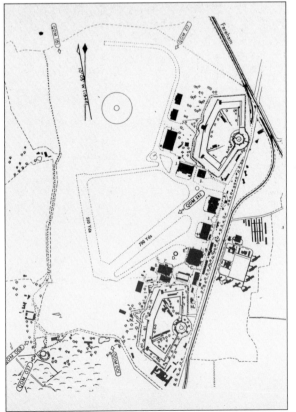

Above:

Gosport: Throughout the war Gosport was almost entirely occupied with naval support tasks and as such was used by No 1 CACU and No 2 AACU which provided target facilities for the numerous gun batteries along the south coast, while the newly formed Air Torpedo Development Unit continued working on all aspects of this weapon and flew aircraft such as the Albacore, Botha, Beaufighter, Beaufort, Wellington, Barracuda and Firebrand. The original runways were much too short for most of these aircraft and several grass strips were used, the longest having a run of 4,650ft (1,418m). An FAA Maintenance Unit was resident throughout the war and was responsible for the repair and overhaul of hundreds of naval aircraft. Despite its second-line role, the airfield was a prime target for the Luftwaffe and was heavily attacked during the Battle of Britain.

Gosport's time as a Naval Air Station was relatively short following its transfer to the Royal Navy on 1 August 1945 when it commissioned as HMS *Siskin*. Subsequently the airfield became the centre of the navy's early involvement with helicopters and No 705 NAS was re-formed with Sikorsky R-4s here in 1947 as the Naval Helicopter Training Unit. Later,

a number of other units formed at Gosport, including No 848 NAS with troop-carrying Whirlwinds in 1952 and No 706/845 NAS which, in 1954, began using the Whirlwind in the anti-submarine role. After the Korean War, Gosport was scheduled for closure, the helicopters going to nearby Lee-on-Solent in 1955 and the long-serving ATDU to Culdrose early in 1956, the airfield officially closing in May of that year.

This aerial view shows the site of the airfield as it is today with the unmistakable shape of Fort George in the foreground and the former aerodrome occupied by the housing development in the left background. However, the buildings immediately beyond the fort, including three surviving Type A hangars and the sole Type C, all form part of HMS *Sultan*, the RN Marine and Air Engineering School. An aviation connection therefore still exists and the training airframes used by the Air Engineering School can sometimes still be seen lined up outside one of the hangars.
The Commodore, HMS Sultan

3 DEFENDING LONDON

Left:

Northolt: Despite the fact that aviation was in its infancy when World War 1 broke out, it was quickly realised that London and the rest of the country were open to any form of air attack and hasty plans were made to provide the capital with a ring of defensive airfields. Among these was Northolt, just to the west of London and alongside the A40 Western Avenue. Construction began at the beginning of 1915 and it was officially opened in March of that year, making it one of the earliest military airfields in the country. Equipped with a primitive lighting system, Northolt was intended as a base for night patrols against the Zeppelin airships, which formed the main threat at the time, and the first operational night flights were made in June by BE2C aircraft of No 11 Reserve Air Squadron.

In fact, Northolt's major role in the war turned out to be as a base for advanced training, although in June 1917 a Bristol Fighter of No 35 Training Squadron intercepted a formation of Gotha bombers over Essex with inconclusive results, the only recorded instance of a Northolt-based aircraft making contact with the enemy. After the Armistice the training function was rapidly reduced and by 1919 consisted only of a communications flight carrying out refresher training, but, at the same time, the airfield was licensed as a joint RAF and Civil Aerodrome. Operational flying resumed when No 12 Squadron re-formed at Northolt in 1923 with DH9A bombers, and in the following year No 41 Squadron also re-formed here with Siskin fighters.

During the 1920s the airfield was considerably upgraded with much improved drainage and the construction of new Type A hangars and other accommodation including what is still one of the RAF's most imposing officers' mess. Also during this period two auxiliary squadrons were formed, No 600 (City of London) and No 601 (County of London), although these subsequently moved to Hendon in 1927.

This view over the airfield in the early 1930s shows aircraft being prepared for an air display. In the foreground are Bulldogs of No 17 Squadron, behind them are the Hawker Furies of Nos 1 and 25 Squadrons, and at the rear are the Westland Wallace Mk Is of No 501 (County of Bristol) Squadron, RAuxAF. A lone Gloster Gauntlet stands in the centre. *QPL E7874*

Below:

Below:

Northolt: In the 1930s the airfield was transferred to No 11 Group in the newly formed Fighter Command by which time No 111 Squadron was in residence with Bulldog, and later Gauntle fighters. However, in January 1938 the squadron ushered in a new era in air warfare when it took delivery of the RAF's first Hurricane monoplane fighters, an event publicised the following month by the squadron CO who flew from Edinburgh to Northolt at a headline-making ground speed of 408mph.

The photograph shows two fitters working on the Rolls-Royce Merlin II which powered the early production Hurricanes via the two-bladed fixed-pitch wooden airscrew. By the time of the Battle of Britain most Hurricanes were fitted with three-bladed metal Rotol constant-speed propellers. During the battle Northolt acted as a sector station (with Hendon as a satellite airfield) and was used by a number of Hurricane-equipped squadrons including Nos 1, 43, 257 and 303. The latter was the first Polish squadron to see action, establishing a tradition of Polish squadrons at Northolt which lasted until April 1944 when the fighter squadrons moved out and their place was taken by the Spitfires and Mosquitos of No 34 PR Wing in preparation for D-Day. *RAF Museum P2635*

Right:

Northolt: As the war moved into continental Europe, Northolt's function as a base for combat units declined. However, the formation of Transport Command in 1943 and the location of its headquarters at nearby Stanmore, gave rise to an increasing use by both RAF and USAAF transport aircraft. This in turn led to a requirement for extended runways and improved lighting and navigation facilities. This work was done during 1944, so when the war ended in 1945 the airfield was ideally placed, with further extensions and a new control tower, to act as London's civil airport until the nearby development at Heathrow was available. Northolt officially opened as such in February 1946 and from then until 1954, when the airfield was returned to the RAF, it was used by most major European airlines and was BEA's main base.

Shown standing in front of two BOAC DC-3s at Northolt in 1946 is a captured Fw200 transport converted for civil use by DHY Danish Airlines, one of several ex-German aircraft likely to be seen at Northolt during this interesting period. *QPL 19231S*

Above:
Northolt: An aerial view taken in 1951 showing the mass of temporary buildings which made up the civil air terminal on the south side of the airfield. These have now all been demolished and the Western Avenue running along the boundary of the airfield has been upgraded as part of the A40 trunk road. The main RAF camp and its hangars are just out of sight on the right hand (north) side of the picture, although that part of the airfield is substantially unchanged today.
QPL 25701S

Top:
Northolt: The RAF had continued to use Northolt throughout its time as a civil airport and it was also a popular destination for visiting military aircraft from other countries. A particularly significant visitor in 1949 was this US Navy Lockheed P2V-1 Neptune (named *The Turtle*) which three years previously had set an amazing distance record for piston-engined aircraft of 11,236 miles (18,079km) from Perth in Western Australia to Port Columbus, Ohio. This record has only recently been broken, and then only by the one-off specially designed *Rutan Voyager*. The RAF must have been impressed as it subsequently ordered no fewer than 52 Neptunes which entered service in 1952. *QPL*

Above:
Northolt: The present main resident unit is No 32 (The Royal) Squadron with its origins in the Metropolitan Communications Squadron which moved to Northolt in 1957. Since then the squadron has operated a variety of aircraft and helicopters including Valettas, Pembrokes, Sycamores, Devons, Bassets, Dominies, Andovers, Whirlwinds and Gazelles. When the Royal Flight based at Benson was disbanded in 1994, No 32 Squadron adopted the 'Royal' title and took over responsibility for operation of the flight's aircraft which are also used for other VIP flights. It is now government policy to encourage more civil use of Northolt and the new terminal and operations complex illustrated here was recently opened on the south side of the airfield to cater for this increasing business. *ASM Photo*

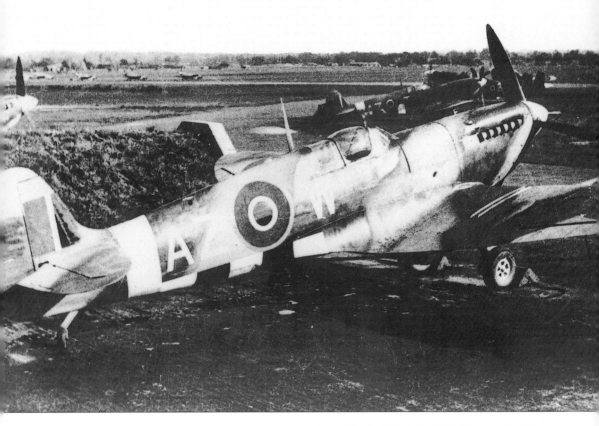

Above:

North Weald: An important No 11 Group airfield during the Battle of Britain, North Weald's origins go back to 1916 when it was first used by No 39 Squadron flying BE12s on anti-Zeppelin patrols. These had an early success when 2-Lt W. Tempest shot down Zeppelin L31 on the night of 1 October. In the following year the emphasis changed to combating the Gotha heavy bombers, and No 75 Squadron was also based at North Weald for the same purpose. After the Armistice the airfield was deactivated until it reopened in 1927 after new accommodation and hangars had been built. From then until the outbreak of World War 2 North Weald was one of London's major fighter airfields with Nos 29 and 56 Squadrons normally in residence, although by the start of hostilities the former had moved and had been replaced by No 151 Squadron which, together with No 56, was now flying Hurricanes. In addition, No 604 Squadron, RAuxAF, was also present in the nightfighter role flying Blenheim Is. By early 1940 the airfield had been upgraded with the construction of two tarmac runways and a new perimeter track, while its squadrons had access to two satellite airfields at Stapleford Tawney and Hunsdon.

During the Battle of Britain North Weald was used initially by Nos 56 and 151 Squadrons; they were withdrawn and replaced by Nos 249 and 25 Squadrons respectively after suffering severe losses. The airfield itself was attacked by the Luftwaffe on several occasions, the heaviest raid being on 24 August 1940 when buildings were severely damaged and nine men killed. After the battle the airfield was host to a variety of squadrons including No 71, the first American Eagle squadron, but by August 1944 when this photograph showing Spitfires of No 234 Squadron was taken, its role as a front-line station was declining. *RAF Museum P003605*

Above:
North Weald: In July 1945 the airfield was transferred to Transport Command and was briefly used by two Polish squadrons (Nos 301 and 304) flying transport versions of the Wellington and Warwick. Thereafter no flying units were permanently based on the airfield until it reverted to Fighter Command in 1949 and was used by Nos 601 and 604 Auxiliary Squadrons, initially flying Spitfire LF16s but converting to Vampire jet fighters at the end of the year. By 1953, when this photo was taken, the two squadrons had re-equipped with Meteor F8s: No 601's aircraft are shown on the right with their distinctive red and black markings, while those of No 604 are on the left. They were shortly to be joined by a famous regular squadron, No 111, which had just received the new swept-wing Hawker Hunter. It was at North Weald that No 111 developed its famous aerobatics team display which broke away from the previous conventional four-ship formation and regularly featured 9 or 16 aircraft and on occasions, a massive 22-aircraft formation performed a spectacular loop routine. However, the disbanding of the auxiliary squadrons in 1957 was followed by the departure of No 111 in 1958 and, after a period of C&M, North Weald was passed to the army in 1966 although it briefly relived its most famous moments when used for some of the shooting for the *Battle of Britain* film in 1968. *RAF Museum P005024*

Below:
North Weald: Ownership passed to Epping Forest District Council in 1979 and it appeared likely that all aviation activity would cease. However, it was used by the Essex Gliding Club and a few light aircraft. On top of this, in recent years it has become a major centre for the restoration and operation of vintage aircraft and is host to the biennial General Aviation Show organised by *Flight International*, as well as the annual fighter meet when the airfield again echoes to the roar of wartime piston engines. These two camouflaged Harvard trainers standing in a blast pen dispersal at North Weald could well have been a World War 2 scene but in fact this photo was taken recently and shows some typical modern-day residents to be seen at the airfield. *ASM Photo*

Duxford: Now partially fragmented by the nearby M11 motorway, Duxford is unusual in that it first opened in 1919, after the hostilities of World War 1 had ceased. Although used initially as a base for Avro 504s, F2Bs, DH9As and RE8s of No 2 FTS, it quickly found its forte as a fighter airfield when Nos 19 and 29 Squadrons re-formed here with Sopwith Snipes in April 1923, to be joined later in the year by No 111 Squadron with Gloster Grebes. All three eventually flew Armstrong Whitworth Siskins, the first RAF fighter to have an all-metal airframe structure. *RAF Museum P020162*

Right:

Duxford: In 1938 Duxford saw another and much more significant first when, in July, No 19 Squadron began to re-equip with the sleek and potent Spitfire, an aircraft light years ahead of the Bristol Bulldogs which it replaced. No 66 Squadron, also at Duxford, received Spitfires a few months later. During the Battle of Britain Duxford was part of Fighter Command's No 12 Group and as well as still being used by No 19 Squadron, was also the base of two Polish squadrons (Nos 310 and 312) flying Hurricanes. It was from Duxford that the 'Big Wing' tactic, conceived by Douglas Bader and supported by the group commander, Leigh-Mallory, was successfully implemented. Each day several squadrons, including Bader's No 242 from Coltishall, would fly in and be

ready to operate in formations of up to five squadrons, hitting enemy bomber streams with superior numbers and firepower. The worth of these tactics has been hotly debated ever since – particularly in the light of Ultra information – but they were a great morale booster at the time. *RAF Museum P015053*

Right:
Duxford: The hangars, shown here in the bitter winter of 1940, were of the Belfast Truss GS type common in the closing stages of World War 1. In their time they have housed everything from frail biplanes, through the multitude of World War 2 aircraft, to the jets of the 1950s. They remain in active use today, housing some of the Imperial War Museum's collection as well as the aircraft and workshops of many organisations devoted to the restoration and maintenance of fighting aircraft from bygone eras. *ASM Photo*

Bottom right:
Duxford: As the war in the air moved away from London and over France, Duxford became the home of the Air Fighting Development Unit (AFDU) which in turn brought forth a variety of interesting aircraft, including many from America for trials and evaluations. One type which spent some time at Duxford having its bugs ironed out was the Hawker Typhoon which was brought up to operational standard in 1941-42 by Nos 56, 266 and 609 Squadrons. The AFDU moved to Wittering in 1943 and the airfield was then handed over to the 78th Fighter Group of the USAAF which remained at Duxford until August 1945, initially flying P-47 Thunderbolts until these were replaced by P-51 Mustangs in December 1944.

After the war the airfield was returned to the RAF and used briefly by the Spitfires of Nos 165 and 91 Squadrons before jet operations began in 1947 with the Meteor IIIs of Nos 92 and 56 Squadrons who stayed until the end of 1949. Surprisingly, Duxford was still a grass airfield with some PSP temporary strips at this time and it was only then that the runway was laid down. This was completed in 1951 which enabled Nos 64 and 65 Squadrons to move in with their Meteor F8s.

This picture shows some of No 64's aircraft, bearing their distinctive red and blue zigzag markings, refuelling during the 1954 Exercise 'Dividend'. In 1956 No 64 Squadron took on the nightfighter role with Meteor NF12s and 14s and converted to Javelins in 1958. In the meantime, No 65 Squadron converted to Hunters in 1957 before disbanding in 1961 when operational flying ceased at Duxford as it was adjudged too small for jet operations. In addition, the airfield had been largely untouched by the prewar expansion construction programme and most of its buildings, including the hangars, dated back to the post-World War 1 era. *QPL 30390S*

Right:
Duxford: The airfield's fortunes began to revive in 1968 when it was the main base for the making of the *Battle of Britain* feature film which, in retrospect, did much to start the current interest in vintage combat aircraft. This view of two Spitfires parked by the camouflaged control tower could well date from 1940 but was actually taken 28 years later while filming was in progress. Duxford is now a thriving centre for the operation and preservation of many wartime aircraft, as well as housing the great aircraft collection belonging to the Imperial War Museum. In addition to the Belfast Truss hangars, a new purpose-built hangar was erected for the IWM exhibits in 1985, while, at the time of writing, another 70,000sq ft (6,500sq m) hangar is being built to house the museum's collection of American aircraft in memory of the USAAF units which flew from here during the war. In the summer of 1996 Duxford was host to a meeting to celebrate the 60th anniversary of the first flight of the Spitfire and the highlight of this was a flypast by no less than 15 airworthy examples.
Ian James

Right:

Hendon: Still on the theme of historic aircraft, one of the world's most comprehensive collections is housed in the RAF Museum at Hendon in north London. This is a most appropriate location since, as well as having been an active RAF airfield which participated in the defence of London during both world wars, it is also one of the oldest sites in the country associated with flying activities. The first recorded flight from here was by Claud Grahame-White, who flew a Farman biplane in January 1910, and by the end of that year he had joined in the development of the site as the London Aerodrome which comprised a large open landing area and several aircraft sheds.

In 1911, with some commercial backing, he bought the airfield and expanded his training school and factory, as well as organising races and flying displays which were hugely popular and did much to bring the potential of the aeroplane to the attention of the government and military authorities. On the outbreak of war in 1914 the airfield was requisitioned and became a Royal Naval Air Station, the five resident flying schools being contracted to train military pilots, and No 2 Aircraft Acceptance Park was established which necessitated the construction of over a dozen new aircraft storage sheds. In 1915 and 1916 the airfield was also used as a base by RNAS and RFC BE2Cs for anti-Zeppelin patrols over London, but no successes were recorded and the scale of other activities precluded any expansion of operational flights.

Hendon was also a major aircraft manufacturing centre and was used by many companies including the original Grahame-White works, Airco (de Havilland), Handley Page and BAT who, between them, produced something in the region of 8,000 aircraft in four years. This 1918 photograph shows the south-east corner of the airfield. In the foreground is the main railway line – still there today – while the hangars at bottom right now form part of the RAF Museum.
RAF Museum P007295

Bottom left:

Hendon

As might be expected, activity tailed off drastically after the end of World War 1 but an indication of things to come was given by the first RAF Air Tournament held in 1920. This subsequently became an annual event (known as the Air Pageant and then the Air Display) and was the most popular event of its kind up to 1937 when it was last held. In the meantime, the airfield was finally sold to the RAF in 1925 and in 1927 it became the home of Nos 600 (City of London) and 601 (County of London) Squadrons, RAuxAF, while in 1933 they were joined by aircraft belonging to the Prince of Wales and his brother – an early manifestation of the official Royal Flight.

Other auxiliary squadrons formed at Hendon during the 1930s but all had redeployed to other airfields by the outbreak of war in September 1939, although the airfield was subsequently used as a satellite of Northolt and several fighter squadrons flew from here at various times, including during the Battle of Britain. However, most of Hendon's activity involved communications flying by a number of squadrons, including No 24 which had moved here in 1933 and remained until it moved to Bassingbourn in 1946.
RAF Museum P017069

Below:

Hendon: Between 1946 and March 1949, Nos 601 and 604 Auxiliary Squadrons were based at Hendon with Spitfire LF16s before moving to North Weald to re-equip with jets. The only remaining unit was the Metropolitan Communications Squadron which stayed until the airfield closed in 1957. Since then it has almost disappeared beneath a mass of housing developments and the only reminder of its past is the RAF Museum which is housed in a building converted from the hangars built during World War 1. Outside, replicas of a Spitfire and Hurricane (painted in the markings of No 174 Squadron) provide a tangible link with times gone by.
ASM Photo

Above:
Biggin Hill: Without doubt this was the most famous of the airfields involved in the Battle of Britain. Situated on the rolling Kent Downs, the airfield's early history was undistinguished: it opened in February 1917 as a base for the Wireless Testing Park which moved here from Joyce Green, near Dartford. The first operational unit (No 141 Squadron) did not arrive until 12 months later.

After World War 1 the airfield was used by a variety of units but closed down in 1929 to allow a major reconstruction and expansion programme to be completed and did not reopen until 1932 when Nos 23 and 32 Squadrons moved in. By the outbreak of war Biggin Hill was a vital sector station in No 11 Group and boasted a recently laid 4,800ft (1,464m) paved runway. Initially the main resident squadrons were Nos 32, 79 and 601, all equipped with Hurricanes, but at the height of the Battle of Britain in 1940 these had been replaced by Spitfires and No 72 Squadron had replaced No 32 Squadron. As it was ideally situated for its aircraft to intercept Luftwaffe raids on south-east England and London, the squadrons quickly racked up an impressive score and by early December had accounted for 600 enemy aircraft. However, the Germans recognised the importance of Biggin Hill and it was attacked several times, raids on 30 August and 1 September causing particularly severe damage but heroic actions by all ranks and some dramatic improvisations kept the station operational throughout the rest of the battle.

The year 1941 brought some relief, especially after the German forces turned their attention to the invasion of Russia, and the squadrons gradually assumed a new offensive role carrying out fighter sweeps over northern France. It was during one of these on 15 May 1943 that the station gained its 1,000th victory, the honours being shared by a Canadian pilot of No 611 Squadron and a French pilot of No 341 (Alsace) Squadron – an indication of the international make-

up of the RAF at that time. This occasion was an excuse for one of the biggest parties of all time held at Grovesnor House in London, but not before the pilots of the two squadrons had posed for this commemorative photo. *RAF Museum P015030*

Above right:
Biggin Hill: In the latter half of 1943 and early 1944 the airfield was home to several Canadian fighter squadrons, including Nos 400, 401, 412 and 485, but by the time of the D-Day landings these had moved out to forward bases in support of the invasion and the airfield's days as a wartime front-line fighter station were virtually over. It still came under attack, however, this time by V1 flying bombs. Biggin became a base for the barrage balloon units which formed part of the countermeasures against these deadly attacks and it was not until October that it was possible to resume regular flying. A few fighter squadrons flew from here until the end of the year when the airfield was turned over to No 46 Group, Transport Command, and was used by various RCAF and USAAF transport units until May 1946. By then Biggin was returning to a peacetime routine and two RAuxAF squadrons, Nos 600 (City of London) and 615 (County of Surrey), re-formed here initially with Spitfire Mk XIVs, but later with the postwar Mk 21 and 22.

The Mk 22 became the standard fighter type for the RAuxAF and the examples shown here at Biggin Hill in 1948 bear the RAV code letters of No 615 Squadron. Both squadrons later re-equipped with Meteors, but were disbanded in 1957. In the meantime, a regular Meteor squadron, No 41, was based at Biggin from 1951 and converted to Hunters in 1957, this change necessitating the lengthening of the main runway. However, the squadron disbanded in the following year and RAF flying activities ceased in 1959. *RAF Museum P013536*

Left:

Biggin Hill: Both before and after World War 2 Biggin Hill was a popular venue for air shows, but, as the RAF presence ran down, the Battle of Britain displays each September were replaced by the privately organised Biggin Hill Air Fairs. Started in the early 1960s, they were among the first of the modern concept of air spectaculars involving military, private and commercial aircraft together with a range of entertainments for everybody, not just aviation enthusiasts. This view shows part of the static park sited on the southwest corner of the airfield at the 1965 Air Fair and features a selection of now long-departed transport aircraft. In the foreground is a DC-7C and a Bristol Britannia of Caledonian Airways, and moving clockwise from them are an RAF Armstrong Whitworth Argosy, a Bulgarian Ilyushin Il-18, a British United Carvair, a DC-4 belonging to Ace Firefighters and a DC-6B from the Italian airline SAM. *QPL F65 23/8*

Above:

Biggin Hill: Used for civil flying since 1959, Biggin Hill is now London's busiest and largest general aviation and business airport. A small terminal has been built around the ATC tower on the north side and several of the old RAF buildings remain, although now used for other purposes. However, a reminder of Biggin's illustrious past and the sacrifices made by its pilots and ground crews is contained in this memorial chapel sited on the north-west edge of the airfield and flanked by replicas of a Spitfire and Hurricane. The former, shown here, is painted to represent an aircraft of No 92 Squadron and the Hurricane is in No 79 Squadron colours. *ASM Photo*

Above right:

Hawkinge: Following the outbreak of World War 1 and the subsequent need to transfer aircraft to France, the position of Kent astride the shortest Channel crossing routes meant that it inevitably became the location of several airfields. One which was subsequently to see action during the Battle of Britain a quarter of a century later was Hawkinge, sited on the chalk downs overlooking Folkestone and Hythe. There are records of some flying activity here as early as 1912, but it was not until 1915 that the RFC moved in and the airfield became an important transit base for squadrons flying to France. By 1918 it was designated as No 12 Aircraft Acceptance Park with responsibility for the preparation and dispatch of all new aircraft destined for squadrons in France. There were no less than nine GS hangars with others under construction and although the coming of peace brought an inevitable reduction in activity, it also saw the start of a parcel and mail service to Belgium and to British forces still based on the Continent.

In the subsequent interwar period, Hawkinge served as a fighter airfield under the Inland Area and then the Fighting Area, while one squadron, No 25, was based here continuously from 1920 until 1938, with one short deployment to Turkey during the Chanak crisis. This aerial view shows the main camp in 1937. Several GS hangars and a single A type can be seen bordering the airfield on the right, while the domestic accommodation – including a rather grand officers' mess – is on the left.

In September 1939 the only squadron based at Hawkinge was No 2 Army Co-operation Squadron flying Lysanders and this left for France shortly afterwards. When the Germans moved into France and Belgium in May 1940, Hawkinge was used as a forward operating base by Blenheims and Hurricanes of Nos 25 and 604 Squadrons, as well as other units later engaged in supporting the BEF during the Dunkirk evacuation. Thereafter the station became a forward airfield for the Biggin Hill sector, but its nearness to French airfields made it a prime target for the Luftwaffe. It was heavily hit during a series of raids in August 1940 and it was not until the end of the year that the airfield returned again to full-time use.

Although subsequently the base for many squadrons engaged in operations over the Channel and continental Europe, it was an Air-Sea Rescue unit, No 277 Squadron, which became almost a permanent feature, staying at Hawkinge from early 1941 until disbanded in February 1945. During 1944 Spitfire XIVs of Nos 350 and 402 Squadrons moved in to carry out 'Diver' patrols against incoming V1 flying bombs. *RAF Museum P015235*

Above:
Hawkinge: Operational flying ceased in November 1945 and after a period of C&M it became a training unit for the WAAF and subsequently was the main training depot for the WRAF when this was formed in 1949. This role continued until 1960 when airwomen's training moved to Spittlegate and the WRAF OCTU went to Jurby the following year. During these years the airfield was also used by an ATC gliding school but this also moved when the airfield finally closed at the end on 1961. Until that time Hawkinge's wartime experiences were recalled by a static Spitfire Mk 9 (MK356) which stood near the entrance to the main camp and is now stored at RAF St Athan on behalf of the Battle of Britain Memorial Flight. The airfield underwent a brief reincarnation in 1968 when it became a major set for the filming of the *Battle of Britain* feature film but thereafter many of the remaining buildings were demolished and today, as this photo shows, there is little sign of the major RAF station and airfield which once existed here. The site of the airfield is shown by the dark field in the foreground, surrounded by sections of the old perimeter track, while in the background only two hangars remain and modern housing estates are beginning to encroach.
ASM Photo

Above:

West Malling: Another airfield which played a role in the Battle of Britain and also in the campaign against the flying bombs was West Malling. Although first used during World War 1, it saw little activity at that time and lay unused after 1918 until civil flying began on the site in 1931 when it became known as Maidstone Airport, although operated by a private company. Requisitioned at the outbreak of war, it became a base for AC squadrons but was later used as a satellite airfield for Biggin Hill and Kenley.

At the beginning of the Battle of Britain the Boulton Paul Defiants of No 141 Squadron were based here but they received such a mauling that the type was quickly withdrawn from daylight operations. During August the airfield was severely damaged in several attacks and for all practical purposes was out of action for several weeks. In 1941 the airfield became a base for nightfighter units, including Nos 29 and 264 Squadrons, and in 1942 the Turbinlite-equipped Havocs of No 531 Squadron operated briefly from West Malling. The Havoc was the name given to the RAF nightfighter versions of the Douglas Boston – although later

the name was applied to all the USAAF's A-20s. The Turbinlite version was equipped with a high-powered searchlight in the nose to help illuminate enemy bombers for nightfighters.

During 1943 the airfield became more involved in offensive operations against Europe and both RAF and USAAF units could be seen here. West Malling was ideally situated as a base to combat the V1 flying bombs in the summer of 1944 and squadrons flying Spitfires, Mustangs and Mosquitos all participated in the 'Diver' patrols. When the threat receded, the airfield closed to allow the construction of a concrete runway and did not reopen until June 1945. During the war the rapid expansion of the airfield did not allow for the orderly construction of buildings to standard designs and this imposing looking Georgian house was requisitioned and used as the officers' mess! *RAF Museum P019848*

Above:
West Malling: During the postwar period West Malling continued in its traditional nightfighter role and was home to Nos 25, 85 and 500 (County of Kent) Squadrons which initially flew Mosquitos and later converted to a succession of the Meteor NF variants (No 500 Squadron converted to F4s and F8s for the dayfighter role). These squadrons moved away or disbanded in 1957 and the last RAF operational unit was No 85 Squadron which returned here with Javelins in 1959-60, following which the airfield closed except for a two-year period (1965-67) when it was used by the US Navy as a base for transport and communication aircraft. West Malling was always a popular spot for visiting units from other air forces as it was easily reached across the Channel and was conveniently close to London. One of the more exotic occasions was an official visit by these Mustangs of the Royal Swedish Air Force in June 1948. Sweden obtained a total of 140 Mustangs from America in the immediate postwar era in addition to Spitfires and Mosquitos from Britain. *QPL 21547S*

Below:
West Malling: Sold to Kent County Council in 1970 and although used initially for civil flying, West Malling eventually closed completely due to local opposition and today is being redeveloped as an industrial estate. This photograph was taken in April 1996 and shows the control tower and the one remaining hangar, a rather unusual J type built in 1939-40. This was a simplified version of the ubiquitous C type and was intended for rapid construction in wartime. *ASM Photo*

Below:

Manston: The depredations of German Zeppelins in 1915 led to the hasty establishment of anti-Zeppelin patrols by RNAS aircraft but night operations from inland airfields proved difficult. A field near Ramsgate in Kent was selected as a night landing ground because the proximity of the coast aided navigation. By the middle of 1916 the airfield was established on a more permanent basis and a number of units moved in including No 3 (Aeroplane) Wing from Detling, and a trials unit from Eastchurch involved in testing the new Handley Page O/100 bomber. By the end of the year it had become the main preparation centre for all new RNAS aircraft destined for service in France and large numbers of accommodation huts and hangars rapidly sprang up on the north side of the airfield. Further expansion took place in 1917 when some pilot training was transferred from Eastchurch, and Manston became the RNAS Southern Training Base for air mechanics and other ground crew.

When the RAF was created in 1918, Manston became home to No 230 Training Depot Station with three squadrons of day bombers together with three flights of No 219 Squadron equipped with Camels and DH9s. After World War 1 Manston was retained as a permanent RAF station and in 1919 the RAF's School of Technical Training moved here from Halton, but otherwise activity was considerably curtailed due to the inevitable postwar economies. However, from the mid-1920s the airfield was used by No 2 Army Co-operation Squadron with Bristol Fighters and the Vickers Virginia bombers of No 9 Squadron. In 1931 No 9 was replaced by No 500 (County of Kent) Squadron, which remained in residence right up to the outbreak of World War 2. Other activities in the 1930s included the establishment of the School of Air Navigation in 1936, which involved the construction of yet more accommodation.

This view of Manston in the 1920s gives some idea of the extent of the main camp on the north side of the airfield and three No 9 Squadron Virginias can be seen in the right foreground. A point of interest concerning Manston is that it appears to have been the only British airfield at which underground hangars were to be provided, but although excavations for these began in 1918, they were never completed. *RAF Museum P004331.*

Above:

Manston: The outbreak of war in September 1939 led to great changes: the training schools were relocated to safer parts of the country and the airfield was transferred to Fighter Command in November when Hurricanes of No 79 Squadron and Blenheim IVFs of No 600 (City of London) Squadron arrived. In addition, No 1 General Reconnaissance Unit (GRU) was formed to fly Wellingtons fitted with external magnetic coils for sweeping magnetic mines in the English Channel and the Thames estuary. The retreat from Dunkirk in May and June 1940 heralded a period of intense activity as fighter sweeps were flown over the beaches and Manston received many aircraft and units evacuated from France. During the Battle of Britain the airfield was heavily hit and extensively damaged during several attacks culminating in a disastrous double raid on 24 August following which Manston was temporarily unusable. Nevertheless the airfield was back in action by the middle of September, although still subject to attack, and it was not until January 1941 that squadrons, including No 92 with Spitfires and No 59 with Blenheims, could move in on a regular basis. For the rest of the year the airfield was a base for strikes against German shipping in the Channel and intruder operations over Belgium and northern France by a variety of aircraft including Hurricanes, Blenheims, Havocs and Beauforts.

The year 1942 was one of varying fortunes, including the abortive attempts in February to stop the German battlecruisers *Scharnhorst* and *Gneisenau* from passing through the English Channel, and operations in support of the Dieppe landings in August. By this time Manston was well known amongst allied aircrew as a conveniently situated diversion airfield for damaged or fuel-critical aircraft returning from

operations over Europe and a rash of expensive accidents on the overcrowded airfield led to the start of work on a 9,000ft (2,745m) runway with a width of 750ft (230m) during 1943. Finally completed in April 1944, even today it is one of Britain's longest runways and is certainly the widest still in use (most current runways being only 150ft (46m) wide). In the meantime Manston became the base for the latest aircraft types including Westland Whirlwind fighter-bombers and the Hawker Typhoons of Nos 609 and 194 Squadrons. The latter were intended to counteract the potent Focke-Wulf Fw190 fighter then appearing in greater numbers and other Typhoon squadrons were also based here at various times.

The German V1 campaign also brought Manston's air defence role to the fore and Typhoons, Tempests, Mosquitos and, ultimately, jet-powered Meteors were deployed to combat this menace. Unlike many airfields, the pace at Manston seemed to quicken after D-Day and it was used by a variety of aircraft and units supporting operations in France and the Low Countries including gliders and tugs *en route* for Operation 'Market Garden' at Arnhem in September 1944. After the war Manston became an RAF and civil customs airfield and was taken over by No 46 Group Transport Command until July 1950 when, although nominally an RAF Fighter Command airfield, it was used by the USAF as a fighter base. The first American unit was the 20th Fighter Bomber Wing flying Republic F-84E Thunderjets, one of which is shown parked on a PSP dispersal outside one of the F type hangars originally built in the 1920s. The 20th stayed for only a few months and the major user was the 406th Fighter Wing, which formed initially in 1952 with F-84E Thunderjets but re-equipped with North American F-86 Sabres in 1953 and stayed until the base was deactivated in 1958. *QPL 25126S*

Inset:

Manston: Reopened as an RAF Master Diversion airfield in March 1959, the massive runway and extensive ATC facilities were available on a 24hr basis and from 1963 onwards a technique of laying a carpet of fire-fighting foam on the runway was available for aircraft making wheels-up emergency landings. However, RAF flying activity was generally limited to SAR helicopter detachments and the Chipmunks of No 1 AEF. In order to make use of the facilities, civil aircraft were permitted to use the airfield and Silver City Airways established a base here in 1959; other user airlines included Air Ferry and Invicta. These and other airlines were often involved in trooping flights for the armed forces and a Hermes of Silver City is shown here departing from Manston on such a flight in 1960. *QPL 41105S*

Left:

Manston: The civil element is now very much to the fore with the establishment of the rather grandly named Kent International Airport on the north-east side of the airfield. This is used mainly by a variety of cargo airlines including several from Eastern Bloc countries and types such as the Ilyushin Il-76 and Antonov An-12 are regular visitors. This recent aerial view shows the civil enclave on the eastern side of the airfield with the terminal buildings and apron at the top. A number of Boeing 707 freighters can be seen, together with several light aircraft belonging to the South East College of Air Training (SEACOAT) which carries out commercial pilot training at Manston. TG Aviation, operators of the Thanet Flying Club, are also based on the airfield using the newly built hangar and premises at bottom right. *ASM Photo*

4 PER ARDUA

Left:

Cranwell: One of the most critical steps in the consolidation of a permanent Royal Air Force was the setting up of establishments to train the aircrew and ground tradesmen which the fledgling service would need for its future survival and eventual expansion. Of these establishments, the most crucial was the RAF College at Cranwell in Lincolnshire which accepted its first cadet entry in 1920. The site already had a tradition of training, having been commissioned as an RNAS air station, HMS *Daedalus*, in April 1916 to carry out pilot training using a variety of contemporary aircraft such as Maurice Farman F7s and the BE2C, as well as various airships and balloons. (The name lapsed when Cranwell became an RAF station in 1918.) Cranwell was also home to the Boys' Training Wing, responsible for training young naval ratings as air mechanics and riggers, as well as several other establishments including the Wireless Operators' School and a PT School.

By 1918 Cranwell and its associated establishments covered over 3,000 acres (1,215ha) including two adjoining airfields (North and South) and housed three separate training squadrons as well as the Airship Training Wing. This aerial view, taken in the mid-1920s, shows the hutted encampments built to house the various training establishments; the hangars and part of the south airfield are at lower right. Clustered round the wood in the centre of the pictures are the hangars of the north airfield. At top left is the site of the airship station, although by the time that this photograph was taken, the massive sheds and gas storage tanks had been dismantled. *RAF College*

Below:

Cranwell: After the Armistice, activity at Cranwell inevitably ran down, but in 1919 a memorandum submitted by Winston Churchill, then Secretary of State for Air, and Maj-Gen Sir Hugh Trenchard, Chief of the Air Staff, proposed that Cranwell should be the site of the RAF Cadet College where officer cadets could be trained and learn to fly. The first intake of cadets was in February 1920 and initial flying training was carried out on Avro 504Ks, some of which are shown here during the winter of 1922. Advanced training was carried out on DH9s and Bristol Fighters, while Sopwith Snipes were later added to the establishment. In addition to aircrew and officer training, Cranwell became the home of the RAF's School of Technical Training for Boy Mechanics and this also opened in February 1920. *RAF College*

Bottom:
Cranwell: The airfield was home to a variety of training units, one of which was the Electrical and Wireless School. This later became the No 1 Radio School and remained right through the war until 1952, operating a variety of aircraft including Wallaces, Tiger Moths, Dominies and Proctors. In the late 1930s the college flights standardised on the Avro Tutor and the Hawker Hart, some of the latter being shown here in a much imitated pose over the completed college building. When war broke out in 1939 the college formally closed and became just another flying training school, but instead of receiving an anonymous number, it was known as the RAF College FTS, at least until May 1945 when it was redesignated as No 17 FTS and moved to nearby Spittlegate. *RAF Museum P008537*

Below:
Cranwell: The airfield was one of the largest in the UK and the flat Lincolnshire terrain meant that the approach and take-off tracks from the runways were relatively free of obstructions. For this reason it became the established base for several long-range record attempts, the first of which occurred on 20 July 1929 when a specially modified Hawker

Horsley took off for an attempted non-stop flight to Karachi. Although forced to land in the Persian Gulf area due to fuel problems, it nevertheless had covered 3,419 miles (5,501km) — a record, but one which was short-lived. However, the aircraft most associated with record attempts was the specially built Fairey Long Range Monoplane and the example shown here is the Mk II (K1991) which in February 1933 flew 5,309 miles (8,542km) non-stop to Walvis Bay in Southern Africa. In this 1931 photo, the aircraft is posed against the RAF College which is still under construction – work had begun in 1929 and would not finish until 1933. The imposing building, designed to emulate Dartmouth and Sandhurst, was officially opened by the Prince of Wales (later Edward VIII) on 11 October 1934. *RAF College*

Above right:
Cranwell: In the postwar era, the establishment returned to its role as the RAF's centre of excellence with the college officially reopening in April 1947 and by 1952 all other training facilities had moved to other locations, leaving the college responsible for officer and aircrew training only. Initial pilot training was carried out successively on Tiger Moths, Harvards, Percival Prentices, Chipmunks and Provosts but in 1954 advanced training using Vampires and Meteors was introduced, necessitating the construction of concrete runways on the south airfield. In 1961 the piston-engined Provosts were replaced by the Jet Provost allowing all-through jet training for cadets. Navigator training was introduced in 1955 and students were taught aboard Vickers Varsities which acted as flying classrooms. The photo shows a Varsity flanked by four Jet Provosts of the college aerobatics team over the college building in 1970. The team was called the 'Poachers', taking their title from the tune *The Lincolnshire Poacher* — the official college march. *RAF College*

Left:
Cranwell: An aerial view of the Trenchard building, built in the early 1960s to house the Department of Engineering formed when the RAF Technical College at Henlow was merged with the RAF College at Cranwell in 1965. In 1970, the graduate entry scheme was introduced to replace the traditional flight cadet system. New entry officers, whether aircrew or other specialisation, are now recruited at graduate level and carry out initial officer training at Cranwell before moving on to complete their specialist training either in the Department of Engineering or at the various flying training establishments. *RAF College*

Above:
Cranwell: As a result of the 'Options for Change' defence review there have recently been some far-reaching changes affecting flying operations. For the first time since the airfield opened, basic flying training is no longer conducted here and all new pilots undergo elementary training at nearby Barkston Heath before progressing to the Tucanos of No 1 FTS at Linton-on-Ouse. Cranwell is now home to No 3 FTS which operates Bulldogs, Jetstreams and Dominies and is responsible for navigator and multi-engine pilot training.

This line-up of the unit's aircraft is parked in front of the two C type hangars which replaced some of the older hangars in the late 1930s. The Bulldog in the foreground is finished in a special black and yellow colour scheme for use as an official display aircraft. Also based at Cranwell is the headquarters of the Central Flying School and the Red Arrows display team, both of these having moved from Scampton in 1995, although the latter will be moving again, probably to Marham, in 1998. *ASM Photo*

Above right:
Linton-on-Ouse: A steady decline in the size of the RAF in recent years, coupled with modern-day pressures for financial savings in the cost of training programmes, has led to the situation where all basic flying training is now concentrated in one establishment, No 1 FTS based at Linton-on-Ouse in Yorkshire. This unit has been based at Linton since 1957 and initially provided advanced training with Vampire T Mk 11s, but these were later supplemented with Jet Provosts and for the first time in the RAF both basic and advanced training were provided at the same airfield. In the mid-1960s the Vampires were phased out and the advanced training task was transferred to No 4 FTS at Valley where the delightful Hawker Siddeley Gnat was coming into service. However, the Jet Provost in successive variants remained at Linton as the RAF's basic trainer until eventually completely replaced by the turboprop Tucano in 1993. Today Linton is home to over 60 Tucanos and provides basic training to pilots of both RAF and RN fixed-wing aircraft, most of whom will have completed some 60 hours of elementary training on Slingsby T67 Fireflies at the JEFTS, Barkston Heath. Although the introduction of a turboprop trainer was viewed by some as a retrograde step after years of all-through jet training, the Tucano is in fact an extremely effective trainer having the ability to fly two typical training sorties without refuelling and a total fuel consumption no less than eight times better than that of the Jet Provost. All the Tucanos are now being progressively painted in an all-black colour scheme which, surprisingly, has been shown to make the aircraft more visible. An example is shown here on the ramp at Linton with one of the airfield's original C type hangars in the background. *ASM Photo*

Above:
Linton-on-Ouse: One of the first of the new expansion programme airfields to be completed, Linton opened in May 1937. Provided with no less than five capacious C type hangars, the camp buildings and layout were of the highest standard and, even today, show little sign of the austerity which crept into building construction in later airfields. Like most Yorkshire airfields, it was allocated to Bomber Command and was the headquarters station of No 4 Group. The first residents were Nos 51 and 58 Squadrons equipped with Armstrong Whitworth Whitleys, and other similarly equipped squadrons based here included Nos 77, 78 and 102 Squadrons. (Experience of life with the latter squadron can be read in Leonard Cheshire's book *Bomber Pilot*.) At the end of 1940 the first Halifax squadron (No 35) arrived at Linton, although Whitleys soldiered on with No 58 Squadron until as late as April 1942. Other Halifax units to use Linton included Nos 77 and 78 Squadrons, but these moved out in mid-1943 when the airfield was handed over to No 6 Group, RCAF, and No 426 Squadron moved in with its radial-engined Lancaster Mk IIs, later to be joined by No 408 Squadron which also converted to the Lancaster. Eventually both squadrons re-equipped with Halifaxes during 1944 and remained at Linton until the end of the war.

From June 1945 the airfield reverted to RAF use but retained the Halifax connection as a Transport Command airfield used by No 1665 Conversion Unit flying the C8 cargo version of this aircraft. However, it disbanded in July 1946 and Linton was transferred to Fighter Command, a move which led to a variety of interesting aircraft and units over the next decade. These included Mosquitos of No 264 Squadron, Hornets of Nos 64 and 65 Squadron, and Meteors, Sabres and Hunters of Nos 66 and 92 Squadrons. Some of the Hornets are shown here in May 1948 while onlookers gaze at an unusual visitor to Linton in the shape of an Avro York of No 99 Squadron. (This aircraft, MW248, was lost in a fatal collision with a Swedish DC-6 near Northolt only two months later.) The last operational unit at Linton (No 264 Squadron) took its Hunters to Middleton St George in March 1957 and after a short period of C&M, the airfield reopened as a Flying Training Command station later in the year. *QPL 21508S*

Below:
Linton-on-Ouse: The airfield's long association with the Jet Provost is today marked by this T Mk 3 (XN589) which stands near the main gate in front of one of the modern accommodation blocks built in the 1960s to house the great number of students passing through the various FTS courses. *ASM Photo*

Below:
Topcliffe: Situated a few miles north of Linton-on-Ouse, Topcliffe is currently used by the CFS Tucano squadron which moved here in 1995, displacing the Joint Elementary Flying Training School (JEFTS) which moved to Barkston Heath where it is located today. The JEFTS was re-formed at Topcliffe in 1994 as one of the first modern examples of military flying training being contracted to a civilian firm, in this case Hunting Aviation, who were responsible for the complete package including provision of aircraft and instructors, and operation of the airfield. With the arrival of the Tucanos, ATC reverted to RAF operation and is housed in the airfield's imposing looking control tower shown here. This was completed after the outbreak of war in 1940 to design 2328/39 and was an early example of the use of concrete for a building like this rather than the traditional brick. The ground floor extension and striking VCR cupola were added in the 1950s. *ASM Photo*

Above right
Topcliffe: One of many airfields planned during the prewar expansion period, although construction work did not commence until 1939, Topcliffe became operational as a No 4 Group, Bomber Command, station in September 1940 – the first residents being No 77 Squadron, closely followed by No 102 Squadron, both equipped with Whitleys. This forlorn example belonged to No 102 Squadron and was involved in a collision while landing. Accidents such as these did much to speed the adoption of standard flying control techniques and procedures throughout Bomber Command and the rest of the RAF.

Topcliffe itself closed after only 12 months so that it could be rebuilt as a heavy bomber airfield, including the construction of three concrete runways, the longest (13/31) being 5,925ft (1,807m). Reopening in mid-1942, it was used again by No 102 Squadron, which had re-equipped with Halifaxes, but in January 1943 Topcliffe became an RCAF base and was transferred to No 6 Group. From March of that year the airfield began a long association with the training role when it became the group training base, and No 1659 HCU, equipped with Halifaxes, moved in and remained here until the airfield was handed back to the RAF in September 1945. In the immediate postwar era the airfield continued to be used by training units including various air navigation schools. From 1949 to 1953 it was a Transport Command base with Hastings squadrons in residence, and from 1953 until 1957 it came under Coastal Command and was used by Nos 36 and 203 Squadrons flying Lockheed Neptunes. In March 1957 the station reverted again to the training role with No 1 Air Navigation School being re-formed at Topcliffe and remaining until January 1962 when it moved to Stradishall. *RAF Museum P016005*

Below right:
Topcliffe: With the departure of No 1 ANS, flying activities began to run down, although communications flights equipped with Beagle Bassets remained until 1969. In 1972 the airfield was transferred to the army and was retitled Alanbrooke Barracks; today it houses 3 Regiment, Royal Horse Artillery, equipped with AS90 guns. However, after being used by various AAC units, the actual airfield is again under RAF control, although virtually all of the main camp, and some of the five C type hangars, remain in army hands. A World War 2-vintage Sexton self-propelled 25pdr gun now stands outside the original SHQ building as evidence of this ownership. *ASM Photo*

Above:
Church Fenton: Unlike most of the airfields in the Vale of York which were opened during the 1930s expansion period as bomber bases, Church Fenton was built as a Fighter Command airfield and came under No 12 Group responsible for the defence of the east coast and the Midlands. Its first residents when it opened in 1937 were No 72 Squadron with Gloster Gladiators and No 213 Squadron with Gloster Gauntlets. At the outbreak of war, when the airfield was transferred to No 13 Group, No 72 Squadron was flying Spitfires, while No 213 Squadron had been replaced by the Blenheim-equipped No 64 Squadron. Although the airfield was attacked during the Battle of Britain, most of the action occurred further south and Church Fenton tended to become a base for the formation and training of new squadrons before they were dispatched to other sectors. Among such units was the first all-Polish fighter squadron (No 306) and the first of the American 'Eagle' squadrons (No 71). By the end of 1940 No 4 OTU (later redesignated No 54 OTU) was established with the task of training nightfighter crews. The OTU remained here until May 1942 when Church Fenton again played host to various operational units, few of which stayed for any significant length of time.

In the immediate postwar era the airfield was one of the first to operate the new Meteor jet fighters with the arrival of No 263 Squadron in September 1945, although by 1947 the jets had left and had been replaced by the de Havilland Hornet-equipped Nos 19 and 41 Squadrons. A line-up of the former's Hornet F Mk 1s, with a max speed of 472mph (760km/hr) the fastest piston-engined aircraft flown by the RAF, is shown here with a group of pilots wearing the typical flying clothing of the time – overalls and a life jacket, with no sign of G-suits or bone domes! Meteors returned to Church Fenton in 1950 when No 609 (West Riding of Yorkshire) Squadron, RAuxAF, arrived, staying on until 1957 when the auxiliary squadrons were disbanded. Other Fighter Command units flying Hunters and Javelins remained until 1959 when Church Fenton was transferred to Flying Training Command. *QPL 24245S*

Above right:
Church Fenton: Although housing several FTC headquarters units, it was not until 1962 that Church Fenton was actively involved in flying training with the formation of the Jet Provost-equipped No 7 FTS. This was disbanded in 1966, but other organisations including the Primary Flying Squadron, the Royal Navy EFTS, No 9 AEF and a UAS continued to use the airfield until it was closed and reduced to C&M in 1975. It reopened in April 1979 with the re-formed No 7 FTS, again flying Jet Provosts, and a pressurised T Mk 5 belonging to the school is shown on display in the summer of 1986 (note the intertwined C and F logo on the tail). JPs were replaced by the new turboprop-powered Tucano from 1989 onwards, these being the first to serve with an FTS following CFS trials at Scampton. In 1992 No 7 FTS was closed down and its aircraft transferred to No 1 FTS at Linton. *ASM Photo*

Above:
Church Fenton: Again reduced to C&M for a while after the departure of No 7 FTS, today Church Fenton is the home of the Yorkshire UAS and is used as a relief landing ground by the Tucanos from No 1 FTS. This recent aerial view shows a typical expansion period layout although only two Type C hangars were ever built, the space between them intended for a third being eventually filled by the T2 shown here. In the background are the two runways – 06/24 and 16/34 – while the concrete expanse of the ASP laid down in the 1950s shows up clearly beside the hangars. *ASM Photo*

Valley: On completion of basic flying training on the Tucanos at Linton-on-Ouse, pilots selected for fast jets move on to No 4 FTS at Valley, situated on the windswept coast of Anglesey. When opened as a No 9 Group, Fighter Command airfield in February 1940 it was known as Rhosneigr, after the nearby small town, but the name was changed to Valley only two months later – presumably this was easier to pronounce! Initial users were detachments of Hurricanes from Nos 312 and 615 Squadrons (ground crew of the latter are shown posing on a Hurricane at Valley), later joined by Defiant and Beaufighter nightfighters of Nos 219, 456 and 68 Squadrons, and these were tasked with the defence of north-west England including the Liverpool area, as well as patrols over the Irish Sea. Fighter operations continued at Valley until the end of 1943 and the airfield was a natural centre for ASR activities, this function being performed by No 275 Squadron from October 1941 until April 1944.

In the meantime Valley's excellent weather record led to its establishment in late 1942 as a Ferry Command terminal for USAAF aircraft making their transatlantic delivery flights (normally via Iceland). As a result, the runways were subsequently extended, numerous hardstandings were constructed, the latest radio navigation aids were installed, and from 1944 onwards the airfield was almost exclusively employed in this role. When peace came in 1945, the tide turned and Valley was the jumping off point for thousands of US aircraft and airmen returning to the United States.
RAF Museum P019809

Above right:
Valley: Reduced to C&M in 1947, although some work was done on repairing and improving some of the buildings, active flying began again at Valley in July 1949 with the arrival of No 20 Squadron equipped with a variety of aircraft for the training and trials role, including Spitfires, Harvards, Vampires, Oxfords and Beaufighter TT10s. When the squadron disbanded in 1951 its place was taken by No 202 AFS equipped with Vampire T11 advanced trainers. Valley's proximity to the firing ranges off the Welsh coast made it an ideal base for test flights during the 1950s in connection with the development of the new air-to-air guided weapons and in

1955 No 6 Joint Services Trials Unit was set up to conduct trials with the Fireflash missile. This unit became No 1 Guided Weapons Development Squadron in 1957 and used 12 specially built Supermarine Swift F Mk 7s, some of which are shown here at Valley in 1958.

The Fairey Fireflash was a beam-riding weapon which required the target to be continuously illuminated by radar from the launch aircraft, and the F Mk 7 differed from other Swift variants by the provision of a continuous wave radar in the nose. Fireflash was a rather crude first generation weapon and was soon replaced by the much more capable Firestreak which used infra-red homing. This resulted in the trials unit re-equipping with Javelins in 1959 and being retitled No 1 Guided Weapons Training Squadron until it disbanded in 1962. Since then Valley has still been used as a missile practice camp, the current unit being the Strike Command Air-to-Air Missile Establishment. *QPL 38094S*

Below right:
Valley: The arrival of the Vampires of No 202 AFS in 1951 marked the start of Valley's present primary role as the RAF's centre for advanced fast jet training and in June 1954 it was redesignated as No 7 FTS. Subsequently the present No 4 FTS was established in 1960, initially with Vampires but converting to the swept-wing Gnat in 1962; these were supplemented by single-seat Hunter F6s and two-seat Hunter T7s in 1967. All three types were replaced by Hawks between 1976 and 1978, and it is amazing to realise that No 4 FTS has now been flying these aircraft at Valley for 20 years, with no replacement likely for at least another decade – surely a glowing testimony to the superb quality of this aircraft. In addition to the FTS, Valley also hosts the Hawk Squadron of the CFS which is responsible for the training of instructors. Currently Valley's Hawks carry the markings of Nos 74(R) and 234(R) Squadrons, and are being progressively repainted in the new all-black 'high visibility' colour scheme.

Seen here is a Hawk of No 4 FTS in the previous standard 'Raspberry Ripple' red and white colour scheme, while a three-ship formation approaches the airfield against the backdrop of the distant Snowdonia mountains.
Malcolm Bradbury

Above:

Little Rissington: Although Valley flew the Gnat from November 1962 until 1978, the type first entered service with the CFS at Little Rissington in the previous February and two of the early aircraft are shown over the Cotswold airfield shortly after delivery. No 4 FTS had introduced a highly successful aerobatics team, the Yellowjacks, using five yellow Gnats, and as a result, the RAF decided to form an official full-time team under the auspices of the CFS (although the aircraft were actually based at nearby RAF Kemble) in time for the 1965 season. Using aircraft finished in a striking all-red colour scheme, the team was known as the Red Arrows and the rest, as they say, is history! Little Rissington itself had been built as a training airfield under the RAF's prewar expansion programme and was selected as a base for the CFS when that establishment was re-formed in May 1946. The airfield was one of several listed for closure in the 1975 Defence Review and the CFS moved out in May of the following year, its component units being dispersed to Cranwell, Leeming and Valley. Little Rissington was then transferred to the army.
ASM Photo

Below right:

Cottesmore: The TTTE currently has just under 50 aircraft available, of which the RAF and Luftwaffe have provided 20 each with the balance being Italian, although aircraft are allocated to the training programme as available and are not necessarily flown by their national pilots. An Italian Tornado GR1 (MM55001/I-40) is shown here being prepared for a training sortie on a winter's day early in 1996. Despite the success of the TTTE, its days are numbered. German training will cease at the end of 1997 and the unit will finally disband in 1998, with RAF Tornado GR1 pilots going for conversion to Lossiemouth where No 15(R) Squadron currently has responsibility for Tornado weapon training. Cottesmore will then become a Harrier base for squadrons withdrawn from Germany. *ASM Photo*

Below:

Cottesmore: After gaining their wings and completing advanced training at Valley, fast jet pilots then pass on to the appropriate OCU for conversion to the type of aircraft they will be flying with an operational squadron. While prospective Jaguar and Harrier pilots will go to Lossiemouth or Wittering respectively, those destined to fly Tornado GR variants will find themselves at the unique Tri-National Tornado Training Establishment which is based at RAF Cottesmore (Tornado interceptor crews are trained at Coningsby). Agreement to establish the TTTE at Cottesmore was reached in 1979 and the unit began training pilots for the German and Italian air forces, as well as the RAF, in January 1981. Its aircraft and

course instructors come from all three countries but aircraft maintenance and other support services are provided by British servicemen and civilians, although the cost is again divided on a tri-national basis. This composition is well illustrated by this trio of pilots walking towards the camera. In the centre is the officer commanding the TTTE, Grp Capt 'Raz' Ball RAF, while on the right is Colonello Antonio Rochelli, the senior Italian officer and on the left is Oberst Dieter Reiners, the senior German officer. To date, the TTTE has trained over 3,000 Tornado aircrew, just over half being pilots and the rest navigators. *RAF Cottesmore*

69

Above:

Cottesmore: One of the early stations built under the prewar expansion programme, construction of RAF Cottesmore started in 1935 and the official opening was in March 1938. Originally intended as a No 2 Group, Bomber Command, station, it was reallocated to No 6 (Training) Group shortly after the outbreak of war and by April 1940 was the home of 14 OTU which trained bomber crews using Hampdens, Herefords and Ansons. Occasionally some of these aircraft also took part in operational raids. In 1943 the OTU moved to Market Harborough and the airfield was closed for a short period to allow the construction of runways, dispersals and taxiways before being handed over to the USAAF for use by Troop Carrier Command. The main American unit to use the airfield was the 316th Troop Carrier Group which arrived in February 1944 and was equipped with C-47 Skytrains and C-53 Skytroopers (both military versions of the ubiquitous DC-3) together with numerous Waco CG-4 gliders. Supporting the US Army's 82nd Airborne Division, the 316th took part in all the major airborne operations including 'Overlord' (Normandy invasion), 'Market Garden' (Arnhem and Nijmegen) and 'Varsity' (the Rhine crossings). The Americans finally left in June 1945 and the airfield returned to its previous Bomber Command training role, users including No 1668 HCU with Lancasters and No 16 OTU with Mosquitos and Oxfords. From 1948 to March 1954 the resident unit was No 7 FTS with responsibility for training naval pilots and was one of the few service units to fly the Merlin-engined Boulton Paul Balliol advanced trainer, one of which is shown here taking off from a snow-covered Cottesmore. *E. Stephenson via N. Robertson*

Above right:

Cottesmore: With the closure of the FTS, Cottesmore finally reverted to its originally intended role as a front-line Bomber Command airfield and was used by the Canberras of Nos 15, 44, 57 and 149 Squadrons. However, their stay was relatively brief as the airfield closed in early 1955 and did not reopen again until March 1958 during which time a considerable rebuilding and modernisation programme took place, including an extension of the runway to a length of 3,000yd (2,743m). This work prepared the station for its new role as a V-bomber base, and aircraft of No 10 Squadron, the RAF's first operational Victor unit, are shown lined up at Cottesmore shortly after their arrival in April 1958. *QPL 37926S*

Below right:

Cottesmore: The airfield remained a V-bomber base until 1969 although the Victors of Nos 10 and 15 Squadrons, and 232 OCU, were replaced by the Vulcans of Nos 9, 12 and 35 Squadrons in 1964. From 1969 the airfield was used by the Canberras of Nos 98 and 360 Squadrons tasked with the EW and ECM role, the Canberra OCU (No 231), and the Argosies of No 115 Squadron engaged on radar calibration duties. No 98 Squadron disbanded in 1976 and the other units were relocated, while Cottesmore was reduced to a C&M basis to allow rebuilding and runway resurfacing to be carried out in preparation for the arrival of the TTTE in 1980.

This recent view shows part of the airfield during one of the annual Community Day events which, due to the international nature of the TTTE, attract an interesting variety of aircraft. Apart from several Tornados, two Italian F-104S Starfighters, a USAF F-16 Fighting Falcon, a French Air Force Mirage 2000 and a Luftwaffe Do128 Skyservant can also be seen in this photograph which also shows one of the airfield's four C type hangars in the foreground and an avionics servicing facility, built for the V-bombers in the 1950s, in the background. Elsewhere on the airfield, a Canberra PR7 stands near the main gate as a reminder of Cottesmore's association with the aircraft in the 1950s and 1970s. *RAF Cottesmore*

Above:

Shawbury: A few miles north-east of Shrewsbury is an airfield with a long history of training activities: Shawbury was established for this purpose in 1917 when No 29 Training Wing was formed here to train RFC pilots. By 1920 the airfield was abandoned and most of its buildings demolished or left to decay, but the rearmament programme of the 1930s led to its revival and it was designated as the site for an FTS and an MU. A massive construction programme started in 1935 and it became operational in 1938 with the establishment of Nos 27 MU and 11 SFTS. During 1941-42 paved runways were laid down and other units at Shawbury included No 1534 Blind Approach Training (BAT) Flight and No 7 AACU. In January 1944 the FTS, now designated No 11 (Pilot) Advanced Training Unit and having a fleet of over 130 aircraft, moved out to make room for the Central Navigation School which held advanced navigation courses, trained navigation instructors and carried out trials and research into the problems of long-range flights.

As part of the long-range flight programme one of the CNS Lancasters, PD328 *Aries*, made the first round-the-world flight by a British aircraft between 21 October 1944 and 14 December 1944. The 36,000nm (66,672km) route was via Prestwick, Reykjavik, Dorval, Washington, San Francisco, Honolulu, Samoa, Auckland, Darwin, Ceylon, Masira, Egypt and Malta in an elapsed flying time of just under 72 hours. The aircraft was later modified to the form shown in this picture with turrets removed and replaced by streamlined fairings (the nose fairing included an extra fuel tank), new Merlin XXIV engines, additional navigation equipment, a Lincoln main undercarriage and an all-metal silver finish. In this configuration it subsequently made a series of flights over

the Arctic, including a crossing of both the geographic and magnetic north poles. The data collected in these flights was of immense value in subsequent years to both military and civil operations. *RAF Museum P015682*

Below:

Shawbury: The CNS was known as the Empire Air Navigation School from October 1944 to July 1949; it was retitled the Central Navigation and Control School (CN&CS) in 1950 when it was merged with the School of Air Traffic Control which moved here from Watchfield in that year. From primitive beginnings in 1937, ATC had developed by the late 1940s into a sophisticated service using a variety of techniques and equipment to assist and direct aircraft in flight and which required a new breed of properly trained controllers to operate it. The school trained RAF and RN controllers, as well as some civil controllers and students from abroad. Shown here are a pensive group of students studying the scale model airfield which was used for some of the training exercises. *QPL 252895*

Bottom:

Shawbury: The airfield had its three runways and many hardstandings laid down in 1941-42. The original plans included four C type hangars at the main camp and two L type Lamella and two large D type hangars at each of six dispersed sites for the MU on the west side of the airfield. Two of the remaining Lamella hangars, together with the extension to the main runway (01/19) laid down in the 1950s, can be seen in this current view of Shawbury. Some of the airfield's many hangars are used today by the RAF's Aircraft Storage Flight which succeeded No 27 MU in 1982 and which holds serviceable aircraft in reserve for all three services. Shawbury and St Athan are the only remaining fixed-wing aircraft storage sites; helicopters are held at RNAY Fleetlands in Hampshire and RNAY Almondbank, Perthshire. *RAF Shawbury*

Inset:

Shawbury: The ATC school used many aircraft to provide realistic training scenarios for its students; types involved included Ansons, Vampires, Provosts and Jet Provosts. In the meantime, navigation training gradually assumed less importance and eventually the last Varsities of the Navigation Wing moved out to Manby in 1963 and the CN&CS was renamed the Central Air Traffic Control School. From 1961 onwards the school began to use various forms of simulators but it was not until as recently as 1989 that all training was carried out without using live aircraft and the last Jet Provosts could be retired. In the meantime, the school had grown considerably, notably with the arrival of the Area Radar Training Squadron from RAF Sopley in 1972. Today the school has a wide range of modern computer-based simulators including this full-vision aerodrome control simulator which contrasts starkly with the crude model shown in the previous picture. *RAF Shawbury*

5 STRIKE COMMAND

Left:

Coningsby: The air defence of the United Kingdom now rests on six squadrons of Tornado F3s based at only three airfields – Coningsby, Leeming and Leuchars. The most southerly of these is Coningsby in Lincolnshire which began its association with the Tornado when the first F2s were delivered to No 229 OCU in November 1985. This unit has continued to train Tornado interceptor crews up to the present day, although it was redesignated No 56(R) Squadron in 1993. The initial F2s – shown here at Coningsby in 1985 – were equipped with the notorious 'Blue Circle' radar, a humorous reference to the fact that due to development problems with the Foxhunter radar system, these aircraft carried concrete ballast in the nose as a substitute. Subsequently the OCU received the more powerful and better equipped Tornado F3 and No 29 Squadron, having previously flown Phantoms at Coningsby, re-equipped with the F3 in 1987, to be joined by No 5 Squadron early in the following year. These three units remain at Coningsby today and the base also houses the Tornado Aircraft Interceptor Trainer and an air combat simulator, together with a major serving facility for the aircraft's RB199 engines at nearby Woodhall Spa.
QPL 85/849-11A

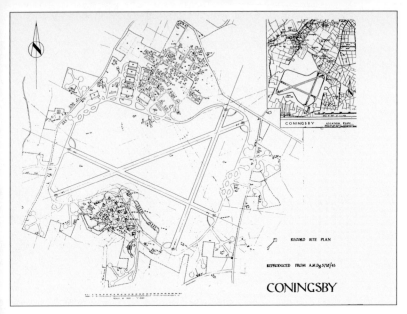

RECORD SITE PLAN

REPRODUCED FROM A.M.Dg 5718/45

CONINGSBY

but in the following year the airfield closed to allow a major reconstruction programme to begin during which the main runway was lengthened to its present 3,000yd (2,743m).

Reopening in late 1956, it was used by Canberras of Nos 57, 9 and 12 Squadrons, before these were replaced by three squadrons of Vulcans (Nos 9, 12 and 35). However, their residence was short-lived as the airfield closed yet again in November 1964 to allow further modernisation in connection with the anticipated arrival of the BAC TSR2 supersonic strike aircraft, for which Coningsby was to be the main operating base. The subsequent cancellation of this aircraft left a vacuum which was eventually filled when the airfield was the first to operate the new McDonnell Douglas Phantom, No 228 OCU forming here in 1968 and receiving its first FGR2 on 23 August. Between then and 1985 the airfield was used by several other Phantom squadrons including Nos 6, 29, 41, 54 and 111.

The accompanying drawing shows the layout of the airfield in 1945 and the main change since then has been the lengthening of the original subsidiary Runway 13/31 (running NW to SE) from 1,550yd (1,417m) to its present 3,000yd (2,743m) – virtually doubling its length. *PRO AIR 20/7585*

Above:

Coningsby: Selected as a potential airfield site prior to World War 2, Coningsby did not open as a No 5 Group, Bomber Command airfield until November 1940. It was not until February 1941 that the first operational squadrons arrived – No 106 with Handley Page Hampdens and No 97 with the ill-fated Avro Manchester. Even they did not stay long as the grass airfield was really not suitable for heavy bomber operations and it closed for almost 12 months during 1942-43 for a complete rebuilding programme which included the laying down of three paved runways and the erection of several additional hangars to supplement the original pair of J types.

When it reopened in August 1943, the first residents were the now famous No 617 (Dambusters) Squadron, later followed by various Lancaster squadrons including Nos 619, 61, 83 and 97. From April 1944 the two latter units formed No 5 Group's own Pathfinder force and remained at Coningsby until 1946 when they re-equipped with Avro Lincolns and moved to Hemswell. From then until 1950 the airfield was used by various Bomber Command Mosquito units but these then gave way to four squadrons of B-29 Washingtons (Nos 149, XV, 44 and 57 in order of arrival 1950-52). These were briefly replaced by Canberras in 1953

Below:

Coningsby: The airfield has been home to the Battle of Britain Memorial Flight since 1976 – originally formed at Biggin Hill in 1957, it had been based at Coltishall for several years. Currently the BBMF has four Spitfires, two Hurricanes, a Lancaster, Chipmunk, Devon and Dakota on strength although all of these are not always in flying condition and those that are are often away to take part in flying displays, especially in the summer months. Nevertheless, the BBMF's hangar on the north side of the airfield, together with a small museum and shop, is open to the public on most days of the year and is well worth a visit. The BBMF Dakota (ZA947), seen here taxying from its hangar at Coningsby, provides logistic support for the flight as well as being an interesting aircraft in its own right. *ASM Photo*

Above:
Leeming: Situated on the Great North Road, now the A1, RAF Leeming is currently a major fighter airfield housing two squadrons of Tornado F3s, although in its time it has also functioned as a bomber and a training airfield. Its origins go back to early 1938 when Yorkshire Air Services created an airfield from portions of two farmholdings. Almost immediately it was requisitioned by the Air Ministry as part of the urgent expansion of the RAF and work began on the construction of a permanent airfield which opened on 3 June 1940. Although intended as a Bomber Command airfield, the first aircraft to operate from Leeming were Blenheim Mk IF nightfighters of No 219 Squadron briefly detached from their base at nearby Catterick. However, a month later the Whitleys of No 10 Squadron arrived, flying their first mission on 20 July, and on 1 August No 7 Squadron re-formed at Leeming with Stirling Mk Is, the first squadron to be equipped with the new breed of four-engined heavy bombers. Subsequently Nos 10 and 77 Squadrons became established as semi-permanent residents, both equipped with Halifaxes, and the operation of these aircraft led to the laying down of concrete runways to improve operational capabilities. On 1 January 1942 a major change occurred when the airfield

moved from the control of No 4 Group and came under the newly formed No 6 Group, made up almost entirely of RCAF bomber squadrons. Several of these, including Nos 405, 408, 420, 427 and 429 Squadrons, were based here until as late as June 1946, mostly equipped with Halifaxes, although the latter two units flew Lancasters from March 1945.

This photograph of Leeming was probably taken during early 1941 when construction of the runways was under way and shows a Whitley Mk V (ZA-G) of No 10 Squadron parked between two camouflaged Austerity C type hangars. In the foreground is the armament store and it is interesting to note the many tree saplings planted around the buildings. When fully grown, these were intended to assist with camouflage and absorb blast from near-miss bombs.
RAF Leeming Photographic Section